ADVANCED RETIREMENT INCOME PLANNING   Copyright © 2020

MW00581119

Note:

*This book is an adaptation of its original version which is an 8-hour CE credit course offered in Canada,
written by Jim C. Otar and edited by Roxanne Eszes of "Learning Partner". More information about these
CE credits is available at www.learningpartner.ca*

Library and Archives Canada Cataloguing in Publication

Otar, Jim C.

Advanced Retirement Income Planning / Jim C. Otar.

ISBN 978-0-9689634-4-9

1. Retirement income--Planning. 2. Math of Loss. 3. Investment analysis. 4.
Portfolio management. I. Title.

Published in September 2020
Second Edition in July 2022
Third Edition in March 2023

To Rita, who tolerated all my b.s. since 1977

       and

To all those who love writing

Author's Preface

This book is based on my research on retirement planning since 1999. It is adapted for the international reader from its original version, an 8-hour CE credit course offered in Canada.

It is a follow-up to my earlier books on this theme, "High Expectations and False Dreams" (2001) and "Unveiling the Retirement Myth" (2009). It includes my new findings since the last one. It covers topics that are important for retirement income planning, but most notably, the luck factor and what you can do about it.

I retired from my financial advisory business in 2018. Here, I tried to include a retiree's point of view, in addition to my engineering background. I expect this book to be my final one on this theme.

I hope you will find it useful and I look forward to reading your reviews.

Jim C. Otar

Toronto, September 17, 2020

www.retirementoptimizer.com

CONTENTS

1 Introduction

Sooner or later, you will ask: "Do I have sufficient savings to give me a lifelong income in my retirement?"

This book sheds light on this question and presents solutions. It is divided into three parts covering different aspects of this important topic.

The first part, Chapters 2 through 7, covers the market **history**. Why do we need to know about the market history? Because history gives us a better reference point for what works and what does not; it sets important guidelines for income planning.

The second part, Chapters 8 and 9, covers the **math** of retirement. Without understanding the math behind the plan, it would be difficult to understand why a plan works or fails.

The third part, Chapters 10 through 12, covers **solutions**. Here, we have examples using sustainable withdrawal rate tables to demonstrate practical solutions.

1.1 Learning Objectives

After completing this book, you should have a better understanding of:

- the differences between a forecast and an aftcast;
- the impact of luck on income adequacy;
- the concept of sequence of returns and inflation;
- the impact of reverse-dollar-cost-averaging;
- how and when to minimize the effect of luck;
- the impact of asset allocation and geographic diversification on retirement income;
- the math of loss;
- how to recognize the warning signals for diminishing luck;
- what is the sustainable withdrawal rate for different needs and strategies;
- green, red, and gray zones of income adequacy
- when to consider life annuities
- income allocation and seven steps of retirement income planning

2 Single Line Forecast

In this chapter, we'll explore the basics of forecast:

- what is a forecast;
- what assumptions go into a forecast; and
- the sensitivity of outcomes for the various assumptions.

2.1 What is a Forecast?

In the context of retirement planning, a forecast is the art of predicting the availability of income by predicting the growth or shrinkage of available retirement assets. For this purpose, we generally use mathematical formulas that are based on the time value of money.

2.2 What Assumptions go into a Forecast?

Typically, forecasts are generated using assumptions on:

- portfolio growth rate;
- income required during retirement;
- inflation rate, for indexing the retirement income; and
- retirement time horizon, in number of years.

Not included in a single-line forecast are:

- fluctuations of the portfolio growth rate;
- fluctuations in inflation;
- the impact of reverse dollar-cost averaging;
- the impact of changing interest rates; and
- varying income needs through different life stages.

2.3 The Impact of Assumptions on the Forecast

One of the weaknesses of a forecast is the freedom to choose any value for your projection assumptions. For example; the retirement calculator on the website https://www.getsmarteraboutmoney.ca/calculators/rrsp-savings-calculator (funded by the government watchdog, Ontario Securities Commission) allows the user to enter an annual growth rate of 35%! This growth assumption would turn a poor person with nothing in his account into a millionaire in about ten years, and into a multi-millionaire in about twelve years by just contributing $18k annually. This is not too realistic.

In Canada, FP Standards Council (FPSC) and Institut Québécois de Planification Financière (IQPF) jointly publish their projection assumption guidelines[1] for advisors each year. In their 2022 guide, the recommended growth rate is 2.88% for conservative, 3.30% for balanced, and 3.62% for aggressive portfolios. Their recommended assumed inflation rate is 2.1%.

To add to the complexity, assumptions fluctuate with the market sentiment: You might use exuberant assumptions during a bullish trend and conservative assumptions after a major correction. In the final analysis, the choice of input can be subjective to the point of being detrimental to your future financial picture.

Let us look at the impact of varying assumptions in a single-line forecast. Consider Paul; he is retiring at age 65. He has a total of $1 million saved for his retirement. He needs to withdraw $45,000 each year from these savings, subject to indexation for inflation. He wants his money to last until age 100. To keep it simple; assume he has no other assets.

Scenario A: After a multi-year bullish trend with good returns, Paul makes a forecast using a 7% annual portfolio growth rate and 2% inflation until age 100.

Question: Will he have the retirement income that he wants?

Entering these assumptions into a retirement calculator, Paul is delighted to observe the following forecast:

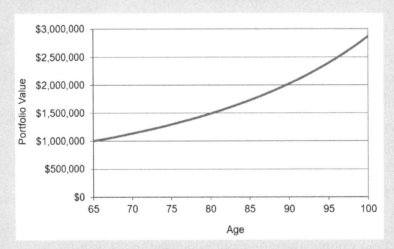

After seeing this forecast, Paul concludes that he will have a lifelong income.

He shares this finding with his two children. He tells them that his estate will have close to $3 million for them at age 100, less if he dies sooner. With this good news, Paul's children start thinking to retire early!

---

[1] For the latest version: https://www.fpcanada.ca/planners/financial-planner-toolbox#PAG

Soon after this, the markets experience a correction. Paul also sees that inflation is going higher. He is now more concerned about his original retirement plan.

Scenario B: Paul decides to make a fresh forecast, this time using a more conservative approach. His new assumptions are a 4% annual portfolio growth rate and a 3% inflation.

Question: Will he have the retirement income that he wants?

Paul runs his forecast with these new assumptions. He observes the following:

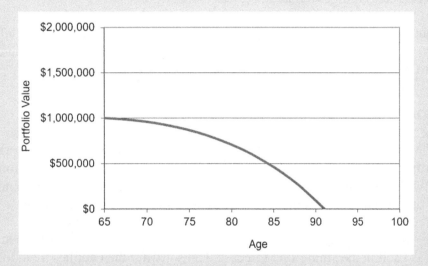

This new forecast indicates that he will run out of money at age 91.

He shares this with his children: Beyond the age of 90, not only his children will have no assets to inherit, but they might have to start supporting him financially. With that worry, Paul's children quickly abandon their idea of retiring early!

What created this difference between the lucky Scenario A and unlucky Scenario B? Two different sets of assumptions.

Your livelihood depends on making realistic assumptions. If your projections are too optimistic, it will not hurt only you, but also your families, dependents, children, and even grandchildren.

When you are trying to decide "should I assume 2% or 3% inflation in my forecast", the number you choose can make the difference between a lifelong retirement income or going broke while alive. The fundamental weakness of a single-line forecast methodology is, that it places an impossibly large burden on you for making these assumptions. A forecast with assumptions that are reasonable today, might turn out to be a ludicrous one, ten years from now.

3 Multi-Line Forecast

In this chapter, we will explore how Monte Carlo simulators (MC) work and their shortcomings in retirement planning.

The longest secular bull market of the 20th century ended with the high-tech crash of 2000. The ensuing three years of negative returns made it the worst crash since 1929. This made the financial industry more aware of the shortcomings of single-line forecasts. Multi-line forecasts were developed for retirement planning applications. With time, they became more popular. With multi-line forecasts, instead of making one set of assumptions, thousands (or millions) of assumptions create a range of outcomes.

While a single-line forecast can be calculated by using only a financial calculator and a few keystrokes, it is impossible to do multi-line forecasts by hand. Instead, computer models are deployed to make thousands of projections in a fraction of a second.

3.1   Monte Carlo Simulations

The term "Monte Carlo" simulation was coined in the 1940s by physicists working on nuclear weapon projects in the Los Alamos National Laboratory. They are computational algorithms (a.k.a. software, app, macro) that rely on repeated random sampling to compute their results. The collection of these results is called MC simulations for short.

Here is how it works: The user selects a baseline, which is usually the assumed average growth rate that was used in the single-line forecast. The software then applies a randomly generated fluctuation to this average growth rate, runs the forecast, and then records it in a database as its first run. Next, it generates another randomly-generated fluctuation of the average growth rate, runs another forecast, and records it as the second run in its database. It repeats this process thousands (or millions) of times; each time, using a different randomly generated fluctuation of the assumed average growth rate and storing the resulting forecasts in its database. When it reaches the number of runs that you asked for, it stops, displays all these forecasts on a single chart, and/or shows probabilities of failure and success of this simulation.

Some MC models apply a single growth rate for each one of the forecast lines, while others fluctuate the growth rate for each age (year) within each forecast line. Some MC models also apply random fluctuations to the inflation rate; either as a single inflation rate for an entire forecast line or for each age within each forecast line.

Figure 1 depicts the results of a typical MC simulation for a retirement projection.

Figure 1: A typical forecast using MC simulation

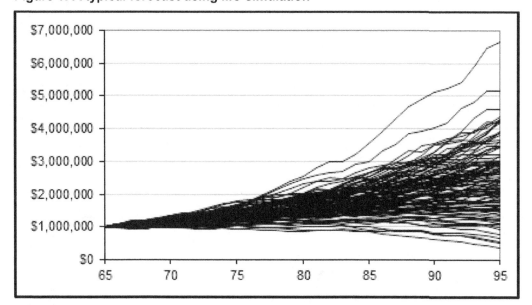

In this example, only one hundred simulations were used to keep the chart not too crowded. Forecast assumptions were:

- initial assets: $1 million;
- retirement time horizon: 30 years, starting at age, until age 95;
- portfolio growth: 8% per year average, varied randomly between 14% and 2% each year; and
- withdrawals: $50,000 per year;
- inflation rate: 3% per year average, varied randomly between 1% and 5% each year, to index withdrawals.

While the MC simulations are regarded as a step forward from the single-line retirement calculator, it also has significant shortcomings. It is important to understand these inadequacies, especially if you are using MC simulators (a.k.a. stochastic analysis[2]). Let's look at some of their flaws.

3.2 Randomness

MC simulations are based on a random generation of assumed growth rates (and in some models, assumed inflation). If all market fluctuations were always random, this would be a great model to use.

German mathematician and scientist Carl Friedrich Gauss published his monograph in 1809 that described several important statistical concepts, including what later evolved into "Gaussian

---

[2] In many academic papers and actuarial reports, the term "stochastic analysis" is used in place of MC simulations. This is because this wording exudes a perception of science, whereas "Monte Carlo simulators" might elicit a perception of gambling; a negative connotation in the financial business.

distribution", a.k.a. "Normal distribution" curve. You might also know it as the "bell curve" because it resembles a cross-section of a church bell.

The formula, or the bell chart resulting from this formula, describes the probability of occurrence of a random event or a random measurement, in our case the annual growth rate. On the bell curve (see Figure 2), the vertical axis represents probability and the horizontal axis represents growth rate. It indicates that most outcomes cluster around an "average", i.e., the peak of this normal distribution curve. As you move further away from the average, then the probability of its occurrence drops exponentially.

Figure 2: The Gaussian distribution curve and the Market

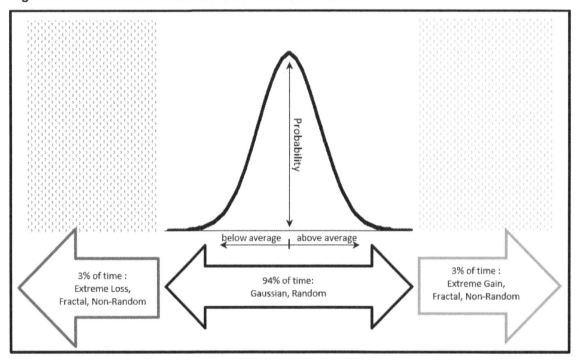

The Achilles heel of the Gaussian universe is "random" because MC simulations work accurately only if the market behavior is always random.

A more in-depth analysis of the monthly market behavior over the last century[3] shows that only about 94% of the time, the equity index moves randomly, which we call "normal". About 6% of the time, the equity index is outside this "normal" (some mathematicians call this non-random area "fractal"). These are the red and green hatched areas on either side of the bell curve depicted in Figure 2.

To clarify the terminology: the word "normal" is used here in a mathematical sense, the "normal distribution curve". Events outside "normal" are not "abnormal", "new-normal" or "deviant"; they are "extremes" in frequency and/or severity that cannot be modeled using the Gaussian

---

[3] Otar, Jim C., "Unveiling the Retirement Myth", 2009, Chapter 15

definition of randomness. Some MC models add what is called "fat-tails" to both extremes of the bell curve to try to model the market behavior more accurately. However, because these fat tails are still in the form of Gaussian normal distribution (but only smaller), they are just as ineffective to model non-random events at either extreme of the bell curve.

Visually, a fractal is how a leaf grows from a bud, the growth of one cell is dependent on the growth of the preceding cell. On the other hand, random is how a cockroach walks on the floor in search of a bread crumb, the direction of each step is independent of the preceding step; until it sees or smells the food, at which point the cockroach switches its mode of walk from random into fractal, i.e., into a targeted-walk towards the bread crumb, where each step is dependent on the previous step.

Within the extreme regions of the market behavior, 6% of the time, the fluctuations are not random. These are the areas of the market where fractal math models are generally more suitable than random models.

At the right extreme of the bell curve, a large upward trend triggers an even larger upward trend as more money becomes available to invest with an ever-growing risk appetite. This can continue until the supply of risk money is used up, or it can create an additional supply of money by elevating the risk appetite further. It ends when all available risk appetite is satisfied and there is no more money left to sustain this extreme.

At the left extreme, a downward trend begets an even larger downward trend, as more investors sell into a precipitously falling market, whether they need the cash or not. This continues until all the risk repulsion is expended.

You might think "Well, if markets are random 94% of the time; isn't that good enough for my forecast". Not so. This would be like saying "I can park my convertible car on the street always the top open because it does not rain 94% of the time". Most damage is done during the remaining 6% of the time when it rains.

In the left extreme region, which occurs about 3% of the time, portfolio losses are large. In the right extreme region, it grows remarkably well. These extreme events happen more frequently (and more unexpectedly) than the Gaussian math suggests. The rest of the time, 94%, not much happens, the portfolios just chug along with average growth, minus management fees (Figure 2).

Both random and fractal regions are part and parcel of the entire market behavior. They are both necessary. Neither is "good" or "bad". They give us hope to make money and fear to preserve it. More importantly, they inject us with the essential -and sometimes painful- inoculation to build the immunity that enables us to grow our wealth in the long run.

Many in the financial industry already recognize these extremes and they promote them in their marketing materials. You might be familiar with statements like: "If you were to buy and hold your investment during the last ten years, your portfolio would grow 8% per year. But, if you were to miss the ten best days, your annual returns would be only 2%!" These "best ten days" they are talking about, are market extremes, almost always outside the random region of the bell curve.

Statistically, the same logic applies to the opposite extreme: "if you miss the ten worst days during the last ten years, your annual returns would be 12% instead 8%!" However, this assertion is not favored by the financial industry for obvious reasons.

Figure 3 depicts various hypothetical growth amounts of a portfolio during different regimes of markets between the beginning of 1900 and the end of 2009 using the Dow Jones Industrial Average (DJIA).

Figure 3: Growth of $1,000 in Extreme and Normal Trends, 1900-2009

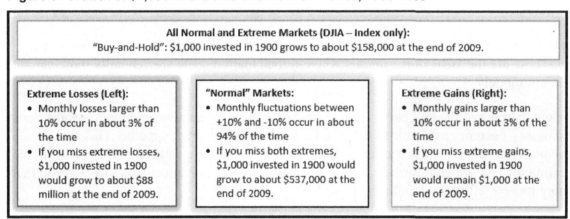

The blue-outlined box reflects the growth of a portfolio that is "buy-and-hold", inclusive of all market activities in normal and fractal regimes.

The black-outlined box reflects the growth of a portfolio that misses both the best and the worst. This means the investor is invested 94% of the time (normal regime). They are in cash in 6% of the time (fractal regime), approximately when all monthly losses and gains are larger than 10%.

The green-outlined box reflects the growth of a portfolio that misses the best 3% of the months of the market, missing all monthly gains of 10% or larger.

The red-outlined box reflects the growth of a portfolio that misses the worst 3% of the months of the market, missing all monthly losses of 10% or larger.

You might be wondering, "What is the probability of *randomly* missing ten specific days (ten best *or* ten worst) in ten years (2500 trading days)?" Here is the answer: About one chance in 26 followed by 26 zeros (one in 2.6 octillion). Compare this with the probability of winning the jackpot in a 6/49 lottery draw: about one chance in 14 followed by -only- 6 zeros (one in 14 million). You have a much better chance (about 10^{20} times better) of winning the jackpot (of the lottery) than trying randomly to miss the worst ten days of the market, or randomly trying to catch the best ten days of the market.

If the probability of missing the best/worst days of the market is so infinitesimal, you would think an average investor would stop trying to beat the market after a few attempts and settle for "average returns". Not so.

In *your* particular case, this behavior started about 280 days before you were born. The determination of one specific sperm to beat 250 million other sperm against *all odds* to create You, is still in every cell of your body. Imagine for a minute; that sperm saying to itself "There are 250 million others like me swimming upstream. On average, I have no chance. I better give up!", then you would not be here, guaranteed. It is in the nature of all living things to keep trying to beat the odds (or "To Dream the Impossible Dream"), even if it appears to be mathematically impossible. That is just the way it is. Stop tormenting yourself for the way nature has so brilliantly designed this magical intersection of randomness and fractal where miracles or catastrophic events happen outside your control. If you want to minimize the impact of emotions on your investment decisions, your best bet is to maximize the use of logic in your investment strategies.

Since 1994, DALBAR's Quantitative Analysis of Investor Behavior[4] (QAIB) has measured the effects of investors' trade decisions over short and long-term timeframes. The results consistently show that the average investor underperforms the index *significantly* year after year. This is partly because the average investor thinks that he is smarter than the average investor and makes the wrong timing bet, usually when emotions overtake logic. This happens usually in two ways:

- emotions overtake logic when markets are already in the fractal region; the investor might say "I am losing everything" (extreme left) or "I am missing this amazing bull market" (extreme right); or
- emotions overtake logic when the investor *thinks* markets will soon move from the random region into one of the two fractal regions.

That is where the financial industry misses the point: The purpose of the buy-and-hold strategy is *not* higher returns. As seen in Figure 3, if you were able to miss the left extreme, you would get an exponentially higher return. If you were able to miss both extremes, you would still get a higher return than buy-and-hold. The *only* time the buy-and-hold strategy would give you a higher return, is *if* you were to miss the right extreme[5].

In reality, the purpose of the buy-and-hold strategy is to minimize the threat of emotions overwhelming logic, thereby reducing the number of wrong trading decisions. The buy-and-hold strategy prevents the average investor from continuously trying what is mathematically nearly impossible, as so clearly reported by the DALBAR research.

While the average individual investor is inflicted with the underperformance as described above, mutual funds are not immune to this phenomenon either. The SPIVA report[6] analyzes mutual fund managers on a regular basis. According to this report, only a few active fund managers beat

---

[4] DALBAR Annual Quantitative Analysis of Investor Behavior (QAIB) Report, any edition

[5] That is, if you missed the best days of the market for one reason or another; either by trading too often, or by second-guessing the market trends, or just letting your emotions to control your market timing behavior.

[6] SPIVA, Dow Jones Indices LLC, a part of S&P Global, https://www.spglobal.com/spdji/en/research-insights/spiva

their benchmark index. Their recent scorecard indicates that, within the large-cap funds, over a 15-year time period, 89% of funds underperformed the S&P500 index. Certainly, this is not a stellar record for active fund managers.

3.3   Trend Types

There are four types of trends in equity markets depending on how long they last:

- Secular Trends: These are long-term trends. They are also known as "generational trends" or "mega-trends". A secular trend can last up to twenty years.
- Cyclical Trends: These generally relate to business cycles. A complete cyclical trend lasts usually between four and five years.
- Seasonal Trends: These are trends based on the calendar, i.e., the time of the year.
- Random Fluctuations: These are the day-to-day random fluctuations of the market.

These trends occur simultaneously and cumulatively: for example, a random bullish fluctuation can occur within a cyclical bearish trend and they both can be within a sideways secular trend.

We will cover trends and their impact on retirement income later. Here, we only want to focus on how MC handles the different types of trends.

3.3.1 Secular Trends

While our brains can handle randomness more readily than fractals, most investors pay too much attention to random fluctuations. We like to attach patterns to randomness, even when there is none. Many confuse higher volatility -even while random- with the onset of a new extreme. In financial markets, fractal events happen a lot less often than the average investor anticipates, but a lot more often than Gaussian math can predict.

The change in the direction of a secular trend happens almost always after a change from the random region to a non-random region (or from "Gaussian" to "Fractal", or from "Normal" to "Non-Normal"). However, it is important to note that not every move from random to non-random results in a change in a secular trend.

To make things even more complicated, the non-random activity can move, like a pendulum, from one extreme to the other several times before settling on one side; hence the worst days and the best days are usually clustered together. Trying to guess the direction of a secular trend by looking at movements from one extreme to the other, is like trying to predict which direction a squirrel is turning by looking at its tail; no more accurate than a *random* guess. That is probably why John Kenneth Galbraith, the irreverent economist, once said "the only function of economic forecasting is to make astrology look respectable".

A Monte Carlo simulation cannot differentiate between the Gaussian and non-Gaussian regions of the probability curve because it exists only in the random universe. For that reason, the results of an MC simulation do not reflect the actual long-term market behavior.

Observe the simulated index value in Figure 4: the vertical axis is the index value drawn on a semi-log scale, and the horizontal axis is time.

Figure 4: Index value over time in a randomly generated simulation

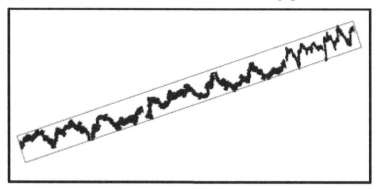

Now, look at the actual market history in Figure 5. It depicts the index value, Dow Jones Industrials Average (DJIA), throughout the last century. Compare this with Figure 4 and you will notice how different they are.

Figure 5: Index value over time of actual market history (DJIA, 1900-2000)

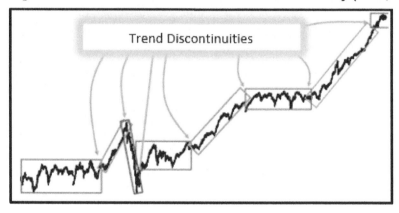

Each one of the boxes in Figure 5 represents a long-term secular trend. Each secular trend can last up to 20 years. It might be upwards (bullish), flat (sideways), or downwards (bearish). A change in the secular trend, i.e., a trend discontinuity, can also be harmful to the portfolio value.

A detailed list of secular trends is depicted in Table 1.

Table 1: Secular Trends, (1900-1999)

Trend	Time Period	Average Annual DJIA Growth	Average Annual Inflation	Length, years
All Trends	1900 – 1999	**7.7%**	**3.3%**	
Secular Sideways:		**2.4%**	**5.6%**	
	1900 – 1920	4.2%	4.8%	21
	1937 – 1948	1.4%	4.8%	12
	1966 – 1981	0.8%	7.1%	16
Secular Bull:		**15.0%**	**1.8%**	
	1921 – 1928	20.6%	–1.5%	8
	1949 – 1965	11.5%	1.7%	17
	1982 – 1999	15.9%	3.3%	18
Secular Bear:		**–31.7%**	**–6.4%**	
	1929 – 1932	–31.7%	–6.4%	4
Other: Cyclical Bull	1933 – 1936	33.5%	1.7%	4

Later on, we will see that "luck" can have the largest impact on lifelong income. One of your most important jobs is to minimize the impact of luck. If the MC simulation cannot handle these important trend discontinuities, then its results will mislead us just as much as a single-line forecast can.

3.3.2 Cyclical Trends

Cyclical trends generally reflect the underlying business cycle. They are the building blocks of the longer secular trends. However, they are more visible in sideways secular trends than in other types of secular trends. Especially during the late stages of secular bullish trends, the cyclical trends almost disappear because of the speculative demand for equities, prompting investors "to buy on dips".

A typical business cycle has four distinct phases: peak, contraction, trough, and expansion. For retirement planning, there are four distinct, important items that change the value of a portfolio: stocks, bonds, interest rates, and inflation. The behavior of each of these four items depends on which of the four phases is currently prevailing, as shown in Figure 6.

It is important to recognize that these patterns, or sequence of events, are not random events. There is a specific correlation, or pattern, between the direction of stocks, bonds, interest rates, and inflation.

Figure 6: Cyclical Trends

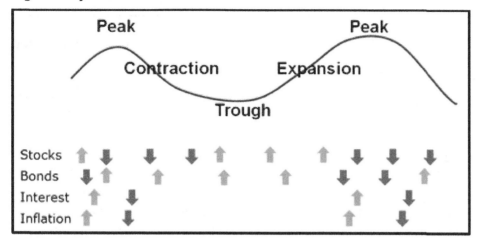

When the MC model randomizes everything, including events within a cyclical trend, there is a one in sixteen chance of modeling the sequence of events correctly. For example, if you run 16,000 MC simulations, only 1,000 of them will likely have the correct pattern for a typical business cycle. The remaining 15,000 simulations will be incongruent with these typical patterns. Because we can never know which fifteen thousand simulations we need to discard, the entire simulation becomes useless.

3.3.3 Seasonal Trends

Seasonal trends do not impact retirement portfolios significantly. Therefore, whether or not an MC simulation is designed to handle seasonality is not relevant to the success or failure of a retirement projection.

3.3.4 Random Fluctuations

MC models work well with random fluctuations. However, as we have seen, the fractal market action that happens 6% of the time, has a much larger contribution to the success or failure of a retirement projection than the random fluctuations that occur during the remaining 94% of the time.

3.3.5 Last Word on MC Simulations

Many users of MC models believe that running one million simulations instead of one thousand will produce more reliable outcomes. This is a misconception. It does not matter how many millions of simulations you run; if the underlying model does not fit, then its results will not reflect reality.

Be wary of any conclusions from any research that uses MC simulations in its analysis.

4 Aftcast

In this chapter, we will explore what aftcasting is and how it can help you in retirement planning.

"Aftcast" is the antonym of "forecast". Instead of making assumptions to "guess" a future outcome, an aftcast uses the actual market history to show what would have happened in the past without any predictive claim for the future.

4.1 Generating an Aftcast

An aftcast starts its calculation by picking a specific year in history, say 1900, at your current age. Using the actual historical returns, it calculates the portfolio value over time. Once this is done, the calculation moves on to 1901 as the starting year. It repeats these calculations for all available years in its historic database. Figure 7 shows an aftcast with only three selected starting years to make it easier to explain. In all cases, retirement starts at age 65.

Figure 7: Aftcast

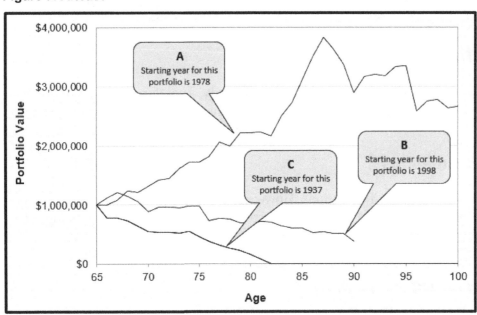

Line "A" shows the portfolio value for the starting year 1978. This was a lucky year to start retirement, as the portfolio value generally increased until age 100, which happens to be the end of 2012.

Line "B" shows the portfolio value for the starting year 1998, which was not as lucky as starting retirement in 1978. Line B ends at age 90, twenty-five years after the start of retirement, because that is when the historical data ends, at the end of 2022.

Line "C" shows the portfolio value for the starting year 1937. It was an unlucky year to start retirement. The portfolio was depleted at age 82.

To keep it simple, we included only three starting years in Figure 7. A complete aftcast includes all starting years since 1900 for US markets. This provides nearly 4000 annual data points that describe the exact correct sequence of events, the correct sequence of returns, correct correlations, and the correct volatility of returns in both random and extreme regions of the past. When all starting years are calculated and depicted in the aftcast, this bird's-eye view of all outcomes makes any shortfall clearly visible.

Planning for retirement income should never be about what happens "on the average" but what happens in "extremes". We all know that what happened in 1929, 1938, or any other specific year in the past is irrelevant. What is important, however, is showing you the impact of frequency, size, and persistency of extreme events. Only then can we design a more robust plan in an imperfect world. Aftcast gives us the essential details to accomplish that.

Let's revisit our earlier example about Paul and look at his aftcast:

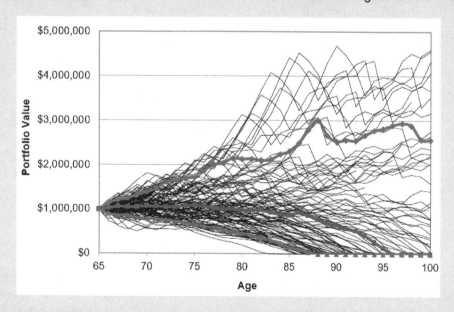

Aftcast for Paul - Portfolio Values

Paul is retiring at age 65 with $1 million in assets. He needs annual withdrawals of $45,000 indexed to inflation. His portfolio has a 50/50 asset mix (using S&P500 as equity proxy), rebalanced annually.

Question: Will he have the retirement income that he wants until age 100?

The simple answer is: We don't know!

Before we can look at more detailed answers, let's examine this aftcast chart:

Black lines: There is one black line –the aftcast line- starting for each year since 1900. For all starting years before 1987, each black line has 35 years of data, starting at age 65 and ending at age 100, sooner if the portfolio depletes. For all starting years after 1986, each aftcast line ends at the end of the year 2021, sooner if the portfolio depletes. Each black line reflects the actual, known market history, as well as all actual correlations and patterns of the sequence of return, bond yields, interest rates, and inflation.

Blue line: This is the median line, where half of the portfolio values are higher and half are lower for each age.

Red line: This is the bottom decile (bottom 10%) of all portfolio values for each age; we call this the "unlucky" line.

Green line: This is the top decile (top 10%) of all portfolio values for each age; this is the "lucky" line.

When we initially prepare this aftcast, we don't know if Paul is going to be lucky, unlucky, or in between throughout his retirement. We can have a better understanding of his probabilities by looking at more details of his aftcast.

Aftcast for Paul:

While the simple answer was "we don't know if Paul is going to have income until age 100", the aftcast gives us further helpful information:

Probability of Asset Depletion:	
Age:	
70	0%
75	0%
80	0%
85	1%
90	26%
95	48%
100	62%

Probability of Full Income:	
90	72%
100	35%

The market history shows that Paul would have no shortfall of income until age 85. After that, the probability of depleting his portfolio increases gradually. At age 95, there is a 48% chance that his savings would be depleted completely, at age 100, it is 62%.

Knowing this level of detail, it is easier to focus on solutions, such as:

- delay retirement;
- work part-time for a few years to supplement income after retirement;
- rent out the basement;
- buy lifelong guaranteed income (segregated funds or annuities, deferred or immediate);
- reduce spending;
- analyze when to start Social Security and any other pension income;
- plan to sell any other non-essential assets (cottage) when needed;
- consider downsizing the existing home, when and if the portfolio appears to be moving to the unlucky area, move to a smaller home with lower maintenance or move to a rental property); or
- any combination of the above.

In retirement, it is more critical to focus on the sustainability of income instead of assets, even though they are related. For that, an aftcast of the "income carpet" can be helpful for a visual assessment of risk:

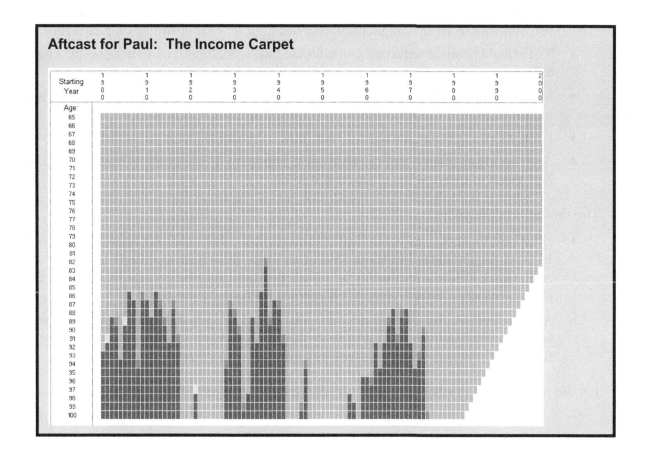

On the income carpet, each column shows a specific starting year and each row shows a specific age. If the color of the pixel at their intersection is green, then you have full income, indexed to CPI, for that specific age and for that specific starting year. If it is red, then the portfolio is depleted. Ideally, you want the entire income carpet green.

The income carpet can help you visualize problem areas. Depending on the concentration and range of red clusters, you can search for specific solutions for lifelong income.

4.2   Benefits and Shortfalls of Aftcast

We can summarize the benefits of aftcast:

- It already includes the actual, year-by-year historical equity performance, inflation rate, and interest rate. You do not need to assume growth and inflation rates. Because you cannot input your assumptions, there is no need to ponder if your assumptions are reasonable.

- It reflects the sequence of returns, inflation, and interest rates exactly as they happened in history, thus preserving their correlation through different secular and cyclical trends, both in random and non-random regions.

- It provides the success and failure statistics with exact historical accuracy, as opposed to MC simulations (which might produce a different set of probabilities for each run).

- The actual historical sequencing of all these data sets allows you to observe the clustering effect of outcomes.

- It reflects both the impact of dollar-cost-averaging during the accumulation stage, and the impact of reverse-dollar-cost-averaging during the distribution stage accurately.

- It allows you to better understand your financial constraints for stress tests.

- After seeing an aftcast, you can then make important decisions about how much to save, how much to spend, when to retire, and so on.

The shortfalls of aftcast are:

- "Past performance does not indicate future returns". For example; between 1929 and 1933, the equity index lost about 85% of its value, from peak to trough. If a larger market crash (say a 95% loss) occurs in the future, it will be invisible to a current aftcast. You need to run stress tests to cover such unprecedented market events.

- Aftcast does not predict the future, it is not a forecasting tool. It only shows what would have happened in history. It takes away the power to input your own "guess" about some future performance. Some may feel uncomfortable with that.

For the remainder of this book, we will use aftcast as our preferred methodology.

5 The Luck Factor

In this chapter, we will explore how luck impacts the longevity of a retirement portfolio. We will cover important components of the luck factor, which are: sequence of returns, reverse-dollar-cost-averaging, and inflation.

For many retirees, luck is the most important determinant of success for their retirement income plan. Many factors can make a big difference between having sufficient or insufficient lifelong income during retirement, especially when the withdrawals are near or larger than the sustainable rate. We can divide these factors into two groups: person-specific factors and external factors.

Person-specific factors: These are factors that are unique to each person's circumstances. Some are:

- living longer or dying sooner than planned;
- unexpected financial needs (long-term care, health care, excessive spending); and
- financial demands placed on you by others (children, relatives, dependents).

The person-specific factors are best analyzed after a base case scenario is developed. Afterward, you can run various stress tests on this base case.

External factors: These are market and economic events that affect every retiree. They impact the asset value of investments, as well as periodic withdrawals that are taken from them. They are an integral part of a properly designed base-case scenario. Here are the external factors that impact the luck factor:

- Asset Value: Two factors influence fluctuations of asset value: Secular trends create **Sequence of Returns**, and cyclical trends create **Reverse-Dollar-Cost-Averaging**; and
- Withdrawal Rate: **Inflation** is the most important factor that creates fluctuations in income needs.

Let's study the details of external factors.

5.1 Sequence of Returns

Asset values change largely in the direction of the prevailing *secular* trend. During the last century, The US equity index grew about 15% per year (on average) during secular bullish trends, which occupied 43 years out of 100. During secular sideways trends, it grew only about 2% per year, 49 years out of 100 (not including the 1934-1938 cyclical bullish trend).

There was one secular bear market lasting 4 years, and the US equity index lost about 32% per year during that time (about 86% from peak to trough). However, a secular bear market can last a lot longer than four years. In Japan, the Nikkei225 index peaked at the end of 1989 and the subsequent bear market lasted 20 years until 2009 when it finally bottomed out.

The largest impact on the portfolio value (and portfolio life) occurs when the direction of the secular trend changes. This is usually when the equity index moves from the random region into one of the fractal regions. This creates an effect called "Sequence of Returns". If the move is in the right extreme, then the portfolio starts growing significantly and this is usually a good thing (for a short while). However, when the move happens in the left extreme, this creates an adverse sequence of returns and it can reduce the portfolio life significantly.

The sequence of returns defines the direction and persistency of the volatility of returns. Usually, volatility alone does not cause permanent damage to a well-planned distribution portfolio. It is the *persistency* of that volatility that can do irreparable damage.

First the good news: You need more than one year's adverse volatility to have a bad sequence of returns. For example; if you were to retire at the beginning of 1987, you would have experienced significant volatility of returns: the equity index dropped by about 30% during October and November of that year. However, this large drop was not persistent and it did not create a discontinuity of the prevailing secular bullish trend. Markets recovered quickly so no adverse sequence of returns followed. There was no damage to the portfolio's longevity. Figure 8 shows the aftcast for the starting year 1987. As it turns out, this volatility was not even visible to the aftcast when using annual data.

Figure 8: Example of bad volatility of returns without a bad sequence of returns

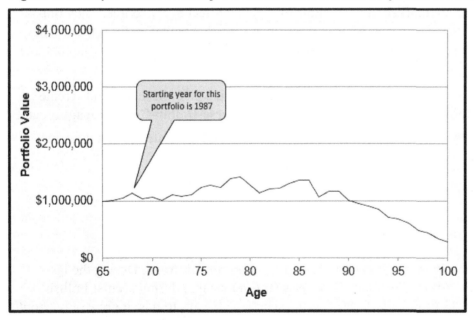

Now, the bad news: Historically, every generation of retirees experienced a bad sequence of returns. It is not a matter of "if" but "when" a bad sequence of returns hits: Will it happen during the early years of retirement? Or many years later? This is an important question.

For many, the concept of "sequence of returns" may be hard to understand. An easier way of explaining it is by asking this question: "Who is paying your expenses in the early years of your retirement?" If the growth of the portfolio is paying these withdrawals, then it is great; it means the market is financing your expenses and you are lucky. Otherwise, you are withdrawing your own capital to pay your expenses. This is not so great in the early years of retirement and that is what makes you unlucky.

Let's look at two hypothetical scenarios to show the effect of the sequence of returns over four years. In the first scenario, the investor is lucky at the start; his portfolio grows by 20% in each of the first two years. Afterward, it declines by 10% in each of the subsequent two years. We designate this as the "lucky start" scenario.

In the second scenario, he is unlucky at the start; his portfolio declines by 10% in each of the first two years and then grows by 20% in each of the subsequent two years. We designate this as the "unlucky start" scenario. Both scenarios are shown in Table 2.

Table 2: Sequence of Returns

Year	Lucky Start Annual Growth	Unlucky Start Annual Growth
1	20%	-10%
2	20%	-10%
3	-10%	20%
4	-10%	20%
Average Growth:	5%	5%

The average annual growth rate for each scenario is exactly the same, 5%.

Let's see how these two scenarios impact the total portfolio growth. First, we look at an accumulation portfolio. The investor starts with $100,000 initial capital and no money is added to or withdrawn from the portfolio. Table 3 shows the portfolio value at the end of each year:

Table 3: Sequence of Returns, Accumulation Portfolio

Year	Lucky Start Portfolio Value	Unlucky Start Portfolio Value
Start	$100,000	$100,000
1	$120,000	$90,000
2	$144,000	$81,000
3	$129,600	$97,200
4	$116,640	$116,640
Total Growth:	16.64%	16.64%

We notice here that the sequence of returns, i.e., whether the start was lucky or unlucky, is immaterial for an accumulation portfolio[7]. In both scenarios, the total growth during the four-year time period is identical, 16.64%.

Now, let's look at a distribution portfolio in Table 4. Everything is exactly the same as the accumulation portfolio, except the investor is withdrawing $5,000 at the end of each year from the portfolio. Table 4 shows the portfolio values at the end of each year.

Table 4: Sequence of Returns, Distribution Portfolio

Year	Lucky Start Portfolio Value	Unlucky Start Portfolio Value
Start	$100,000	$100,000
1	$115,000	$85,000
2	$133,000	$71,500
3	$114,700	$80,800
4	$98,230	$91,960
Net Reduction:	1.77%	8.04%

Lucky Start: When the investor has a lucky start, the growth of the portfolio paid his withdrawals entirely during the first three years. Only in the fourth year did he have to dip into his original capital slightly. The net decrease over this four-year time period, including his withdrawals, was 1.77%.

Unlucky Start: For the unlucky retiree, his withdrawals were paid entirely by his own original capital during the first two years of his retirement. This created permanent damage. During the following two years, withdrawals were paid entirely by the growth, but this did not repair the damage done in the first two years. The net decrease of the portfolio value over this four-year time period was much larger than for the lucky retiree, 8.04%.

This example shows only four years. Remember that secular trends can last up to twenty years, and a bad sequence of returns can create conditions where the retiree must dip into his own capital for several years. When the retiree is this unlucky, conventional strategies like asset allocation and diversification are largely ineffective, as we will see in upcoming chapters.

To protect income, other remedies such as keeping the withdrawals below the sustainable rate, or pooling the risk for lifelong guaranteed income (insurance products), are effective ways of minimizing the impact of the sequence of returns.

---

[7] Keep in mind; portfolio costs and MER's also count as withdrawals from a portfolio. Therefore, sequence of returns impacts the total growth in accumulation portfolios too, especially if periodically added amounts are less than portfolio costs and MER's. However, it is outside the scope of our discussion here.

If you still have a hard time understanding the concept of sequence of returns, here is an easier explanation:

- Accumulation stage: If you are adding money to the portfolio, it does *not matter* how you line up the accumulations: "2 + 1" is the same as "1 + 2"; and

- Distribution stage: If you are removing money from the portfolio, it *does matter* how you line up the withdrawals: "2 - 1" is *not* the same as "1 - 2".

5.2 Reverse Dollar Cost Averaging

Cyclical trends create fluctuations in asset values. They usually do so in the random region of the probability curve. While the effect on the portfolio value is less damaging than a secular trend, it creates "Reverse-Dollar-Cost-Averaging" (RDCA). If the withdrawal plan is designed improperly, then RDCA can reduce the portfolio life.

First, what is dollar-cost-averaging (DCA)? When a constant amount of money is added to a fluctuating investment periodically, it buys a larger number of shares when the share price is low, and fewer shares when it is high. Therefore, the average cost is always lower than the average market price of shares after a recovery from a cyclical trend. Therefore, DCA is an effective strategy for accumulation portfolios with fluctuating asset values.

Here is a DCA example:

Dollar-Cost Averaging Example:

Brian has $10,000 in his portfolio. He is planning to add $600 each month to his investment. The current share price is $10.

Next month, the share price drops to $7. After hitting that low point, the share price gradually recovers back to $10.

The following table shows the activity in the account:

Month	Share Price	Dollar Amount	Cumulative Cost	Shares traded	Share Balance	Market Value
Start	$10.00	$10,000	$10,000	1,000.00	1,000.00	$10,000
1	$7.00	$600	$10,600	85.71	1,085.71	$7,600
2	$8.00	$600	$11,200	75.00	1,160.71	$9,286
3	$9.00	$600	$11,800	66.67	1,227.38	$11,046
4	$10.00	$600	$12,400	60.00	1,287.38	$12,874

...continued on the next page

The monthly $600 investment bought a larger number of shares when the price was low, and fewer as the price was rising. When the share price went back to $10, Brian had more shares in his portfolio to participate in this rise. At the end of this cycle, even though the share price was exactly the same as it was at the start of the cycle, his cumulative cost was $12,400 and the total market value of his portfolio was $12,874.

Therefore, Brian's net gain attributable to DCA is 3.8%, calculated as [($12,874 − $12,400) / $12,400] x 100%

In a distribution portfolio, reverse dollar-cost averaging (RDCA) works exactly in the opposite way. Investments are sold periodically to provide an income. During a bear market, you need to sell more shares at a lower price to deliver the same dollar amount of income to the retiree. Once these shares have been sold, they are no longer in the portfolio. Now, fewer number of shares bear the burden of recovering afterward. Here is an RDCA example:

Reverse-Dollar-Cost Averaging Example:

Ed has $10,000 in his portfolio. He is withdrawing $600 each month. The current share price is $10.

The following month, the share price drops to $7. After hitting that low point, the share price gradually recovers back to $10.

The following table shows the activity in the account:

Month	Share Price	Dollar Amount	Cumulative Cost	Shares traded	Share Balance	Market Value
Start	$10.00	$10,000	$10,000	1,000.00	1,000.00	$10,000
1	$7.00	($600)	$9,400	(85.71)	914.29	$6,400
2	$8.00	($600)	$8,800	(75.00)	839.29	$6,714
3	$9.00	($600)	$8,200	(66.67)	772.62	$6,954
4	$10.00	($600)	$7,600	(60.00)	712.62	$7,126

Unfortunately, for the same $600 monthly income, Ed was forced to sell more shares when the price was lower. As the share price was recovering, he had fewer and fewer shares in his portfolio to participate in this rise. At the end of this cycle, even though the share price was exactly the same as it was at the start of the cycle, his cumulative cost was $7,600 and the total market value is $7,126.

Therefore, Ed's net loss attributable to RDCA is 6.2%, calculated as [($7,126 / $7,600) − 1] x 100%

It is important to differentiate between the impact of sequence of returns and RDCA on a retirement portfolio:

- Sequence of returns is related to changes in *secular trends* and caused by the persistence of adverse volatility. You might have high volatility but if it is not persistent, there is no bad sequence of returns and no permanent damage.
- On the other hand, RDCA is related to *cyclical* trends and caused by any type of volatility, persistent or not. If withdrawals are made from fluctuating investments, then permanent damage will occur.

The good news is, that you can absolutely eliminate RDCA. When withdrawals are generated from investments that do not fluctuate in value, RDCA disappears completely; there is no damage at all. Two of the most effective ways of accomplishing this are:

- a proper asset allocation: maintain a cash "bucket" (or money market, or short-term bond fund) to cover withdrawals fully over a typical business cycle (about five years of withdrawals), and
- a proper withdrawal strategy: stop reinvesting dividends/distributions generated from investments in the portfolio. Instead, collect any dividends/distributions in cash, and add these to the cash "bucket" to use for withdrawals.

Some might ask "if the cash bucket strategy works for RDCA, why not use it for the sequence of returns too?" Answer: It won't work. This is because once withdrawals exceed sustainable levels, which can happen after only one episode of a bad sequence of returns, the time horizon of the *investor* and the time horizon of the *portfolio* disconnect. After this "point of no return", the time horizon of the investor becomes irrelevant. Even if the investor was willing to wait "forever", it would not prevent the portfolio's eventual depletion.

5.3 Inflation

After the sequence of returns, inflation has the largest impact on portfolio longevity. It forces the retiree to adjust withdrawals, usually higher, throughout retirement.

While the sequence of returns impacts only the portfolio value, inflation impacts withdrawals directly. If you experience high inflation even for a very short time, say a couple of years, your withdrawals will be higher for the rest of your life.

Also, to fight higher inflation, central banks increase short–term interest rates. This ultimately pushes down share prices, which can create a new episode of a bad sequence of returns. The net effect of this one-two punch is, that the retiree is forced to withdraw increasingly larger amounts from his investments and he must do so from a shrinking asset base.

Figure 9 shows inflation over the last century in the USA[8].

---

[8] U.S. Bureau of Labor Statistics, wholesale price index for the years 1900–1913, the consumer price index after 1913.

Figure 9: Inflation, 1900-2022

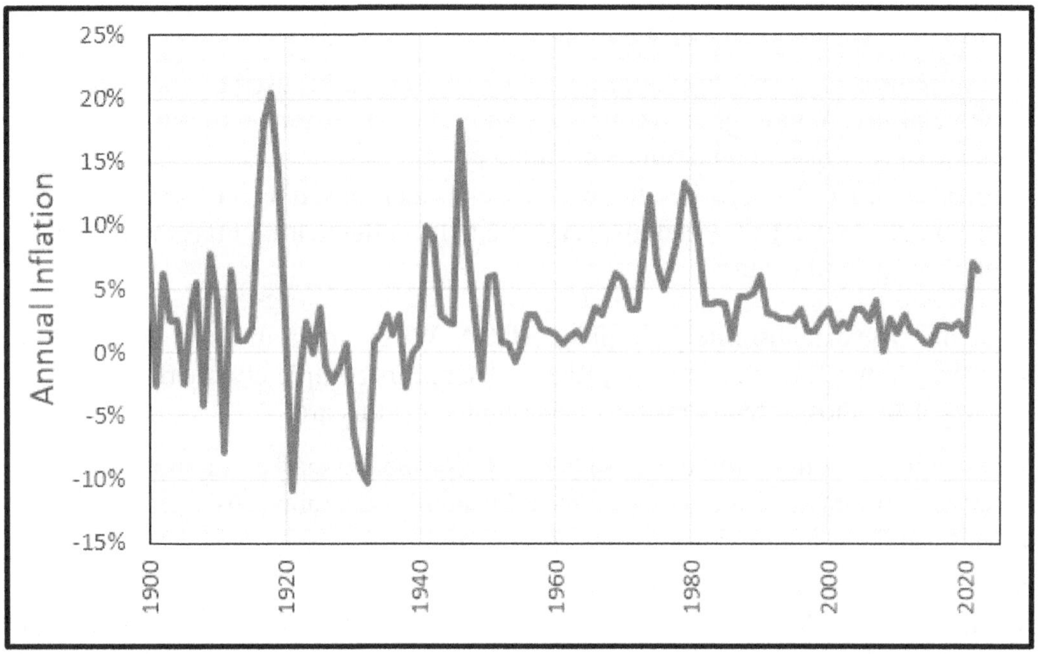

When we observe inflation rates in different secular trends for the US markets as shown earlier in Table 1, we notice:

- In secular bullish trends, the average inflation was 1.8%. Compare this with the 15% average growth of equities and you have the definition of the "lucky" retiree;

- In secular sideways trends (about half of the last century), the average inflation was 5.6%, which is much higher than in secular bullish trends. Compare this with the 2.4% average growth in equities, you have the definition of the "unlucky" retiree; and

- In the only secular bearish trend, between 1929 and 1933, there was no inflation problem. However, the concern in a secular bear market is not inflation or deflation, but devastating losses.

One of the common misconceptions indoctrinated by the financial industry is, that equities always beat inflation. This is not entirely correct. They beat inflation during secular bullish trends; however, outside of that, they usually don't.

Figure 10 shows the increase of the equity index and inflation from start to finish of each secular bullish trend. In all cases, the equities were able to beat the index, as expected.

Figure 11 shows the same chart with only sideways and bearish secular trends. The equity index did not beat inflation for the entire trend.

Figure 10: Inflation and Equity Indices during Secular Bullish Trends

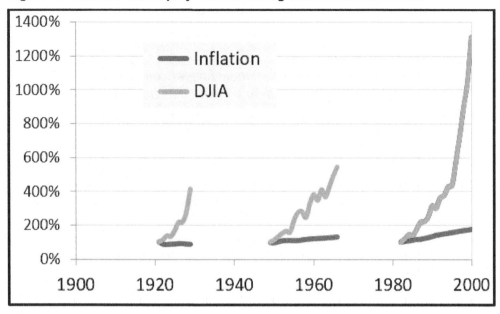

Figure 11: Inflation and Equity Indices during Secular Sideways and Bearish Trends

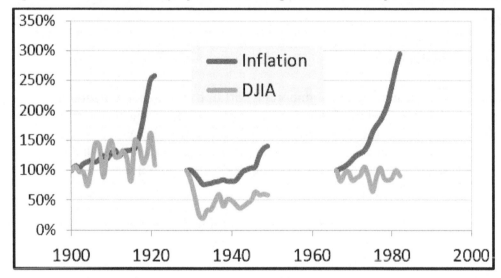

Inflation impacts you the most if you are already retired. If you are still earning income from work or business, it has much less impact.

One of the strategies to minimize the impact of an unexpected spike in the inflation rate during retirement is to purchase a guaranteed income stream. It eliminates market and longevity risks. This will allow the retiree to use his remaining investment portfolio as an inflation "bucket" for inflation protection only. We will discuss these strategies later.

6 The Impact of Asset Allocation

In this chapter, we will explore the impact of asset allocation on a retirement portfolio.

> *"Research has shown that asset allocation is the single largest contributor to a portfolio's success. It is much more important than security selection. In fact, one study concluded that asset allocation accounted for over 90% of the difference in a portfolio's investment return."*

Different variations of this statement appear in articles, sales brochures, and newsletters in the financial media. It is based on what is known as the Brinson Study[9]. This research analyzed data from 91 large corporate pension plans with assets of at least $100 million over a 10–year period beginning in 1974. It concluded that the contributors to the difference in the success of a portfolio are:

- asset allocation: 93.6%;
- security selection 2.5%;
- other: 2.2%; and
- market timing 1.7%.

The Brinson study measured the success of a portfolio by the impact of each of these factors on the growth rate of the portfolio.

6.1 Distribution Portfolios

There is no doubt that asset allocation is a very important part of portfolio construction in accumulation portfolios, which is what the Brinson study explored. However, when it comes to distribution portfolios (retirement portfolios) there are two additional vital factors: sequence of returns and inflation. Because the impact of these two factors is not explicitly included in the Brinson study, we cannot take the findings of the Brinson study and apply them to distribution portfolios.

During the accumulation stage, the *growth rate of a portfolio* might be the most important objective. However, during the distribution stage, the most important objective -unequivocally- is the *sustainability of income*. Asset allocation might be a significant factor during accumulation, but income allocation (or how lifelong income is generated) is the most significant factor during retirement.

When a bad sequence of returns or a bout of high inflation decreases the portfolio life from 35 years to 18 years, the sustainability of income -perhaps through guaranteed income- should be your prime concern, not whether you should allocate 52% or 63% to your equities.

---

[9] "Determinants of Portfolio Performance II," by Gary P. Brinson, Randolph L. Hood, and Gilbert L Beebower, Financial Analysts Journal, January/February 1995. This was a follow–up study to their original one in 1986.

Specifically, here are the reasons why the Brinson study does not apply to distribution portfolios of individual retirees:

- The dynamics of cash flow in a pension fund are entirely different from the dynamics of cash flow in an individual retirement account. When there is a shortfall in a pension fund, contributions are increased to meet this shortfall. A pension fund is an "open–perpetual" system; an individual retirement account is a "closed–finite" system.

- A pension fund has a continuous inflow of money over time. In an individual retirement account, the inflow of money occurs usually until retirement. After that, there is no more inflow, but only outflow.

- Total portfolio costs of pension funds and individual retirement portfolios are vastly different. This makes a big difference over time.

- In an individual retirement account, once withdrawals start, the effect of the "sequence of returns" can be devastating. During the time period of the Brinson study, there was a continuous inflow of money with no perceivable impact from the sequence of returns.

- In an individual retirement account, once withdrawals start, the effect of "reverse dollar–cost–averaging" can be important. In a pension fund, since there is a continuous inflow of money, this creates a dollar-cost-averaging, which actually enhances the portfolio growth.

- In an individual account, inflation is important. Withdrawals must be increased over time to maintain the purchasing power of the retiree. In pension funds, there is no such concern; as inflation goes up, salaries also go up and pension contributions increase as well. This cushions the effect of inflation in the pension fund.

- The twenty-year time frame of the study is too short. It rides on a single secular bullish trend, arguably the luckiest time period of the last century. Such a short time frame misses significant fractal events that come with trend discontinuities, as shown in Figure 12.

Figure 12: Period covered in the Brinson study

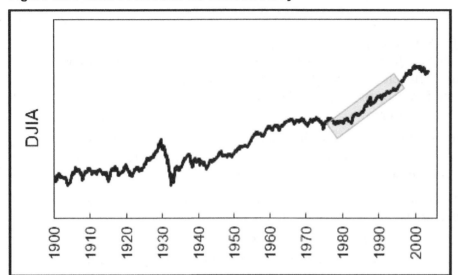

6.2 Asset Allocation Scenarios

We can study the impact of asset allocation by looking at three different scenarios. The following is common to all three scenarios:

- each person is 65 years old and retiring now;
- income is required until age 96;
- retirement savings are valued at $1 million;
- equities pay an average dividend of 2%;
- the equity proxy is S&P500;
- fixed income portion of the portfolio returns 1.5% over and above the historical 6-month CD rates;
- the portfolio management costs are 1% of the portfolio value; and
- the asset mix is rebalanced annually.

6.2.1 Scenario A – Withdrawals Larger than the Sustainable Withdrawal Rate

In Scenario A, Marilyn needs $60,000/year, which is significantly larger than her sustainable withdrawal rate.

Scenario A1: The Buy-and-Hold Strategy

Figure 13 shows the aftcast for the 50% equity and 50% fixed income asset mix, using a buy-and-hold strategy.

Figure 13: Aftcast for Marilyn, 50/50 asset mix

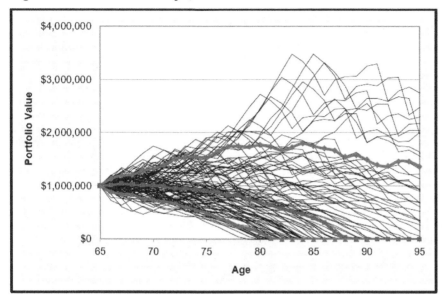

Keep in mind; that for a retiree, the most important thing is the portfolio longevity and not the growth of the portfolio. To study the impact of asset allocation, we varied the asset allocation and noted the range of shortest and longest portfolio life in Figure 14. The vertical axis shows the range of the portfolio life. The horizontal axis shows three different asset mixes.

Figure 14: Marilyn's Portfolio Life for various asset mixes

Figure 14 shows that asset allocation had no noticeable impact on the minimum portfolio life in this particular scenario. If she was unlucky, she ran out of income as early as twelve years after retirement, regardless of the asset mix. If she was lucky, she had income for forty years or more. All else being equal, any variation of the portfolio life was attributable only to the luck factor.

Scenario A2: Age-based Asset Allocation Strategy

Marilyn heard somewhere about age-based asset allocation. According to this strategy, she would allocate the same percentage as her age to her fixed income holdings: at age 65, she allocates 65% to fixed income and the remainder 35% to equities. At age 75, she allocates 75% to fixed income and the remainder of 25% to equities, and so on. With this strategy, as she gets older, her portfolio becomes more conservative.

Does this strategy improve the outcome? The answer is shown in the fourth column of Figure 15: In the worst case, the shortest portfolio life was thirteen years, the same as using a 30/70 or a 50/50 "buy-and-hold" asset mix. Thus, the age-based asset allocation strategy did not improve the outcome.

Figure 15: Marilyn's Portfolio Life for various asset mixes and strategies

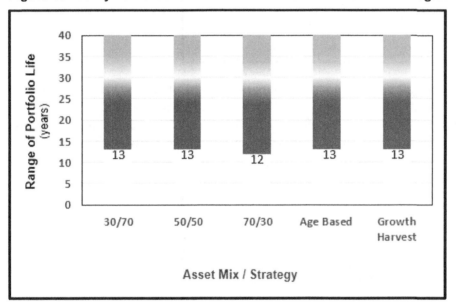

Scenario A3: Growth Harvesting Strategy

Marilyn tries a different strategy, called "growth harvesting". Here is how this strategy works: She starts with a 50/50 asset mix. Each year, if the equity index grows by more than 8%, she cashes out the growth of the portfolio and adds this to her cash bucket. She withdraws her retirement income from this cash bucket over time. With this strategy, she takes advantage of the above-average growth of her equity holdings when that happens.

As we see in the fifth column of Figure 15, this strategy does not help her either. In the worst case, the shortest portfolio life was thirteen years, the same as using a 30/70 or a 50/50 asset mix under the "buy-and-hold" asset mix.

Conclusion

When the withdrawal rate is larger than the sustainable withdrawal rate, asset allocation strategies do not increase portfolio longevity in any significant way. Do not waste your time trying to find some magic cure by playing with asset allocation, rebalancing, growth harvesting, bucket strategies, adaptive withdrawals, market timing, and so on. None can fix this shortfall. You need to consider other approaches:

- Change personal parameters: delay retirement, spend less, generate extra income during early years of retirement, downsize home, rent part of the home, etc.; and
- Reduce risk: buy guaranteed lifelong income, such as life annuities or variable annuities with income guarantees.

6.2.2 Scenario B – Withdrawals are near the Sustainable Withdrawal Rate

In Scenario B, Bill needs $40,000/ year, which is slightly larger than the sustainable withdrawal rate. The portfolio life for three different asset mixes using a buy-and-hold strategy is depicted in Figure 16.

Figure 16: Bill's Portfolio Life for various asset mixes

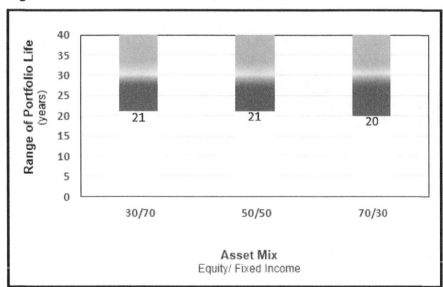

In Bill's case, the worst-case portfolio life was better than Marilyn's, only because of the lower withdrawal rate. Asset allocation did not have any significant impact on the worst-case portfolio life.

However, the aftcast revealed additional information: While the asset mix did not impact the worst-case portfolio life, it made a difference in the probability of being lucky. At 30/70 asset mix, the probability of lifelong income was 90%, at 50/50 it was 83%, and at 70/30 it was 76%.

Therefore, for Bill, while asset allocation does not alleviate the problem of the worst-case portfolio life, an asset allocation of 30% equity and 70% fixed income gave the best "average" success rate.

In scenarios like this, where the withdrawal rate is near sustainable, think about allocating some of the retirement assets to purchase guaranteed income for covering essential expenses. Or consider delaying retirement, reducing spending, and generating extra income during the early years of retirement, as these will also help to remedy most such situations.

6.2.3 Scenario C – Withdrawals are below the Sustainable Withdrawal Rate

Jane needs $20,000/year, which is well below the sustainable withdrawal rate. The aftcast is depicted in Figure 17.

Figure 17: Aftcast for Jane, 50/50 asset mix

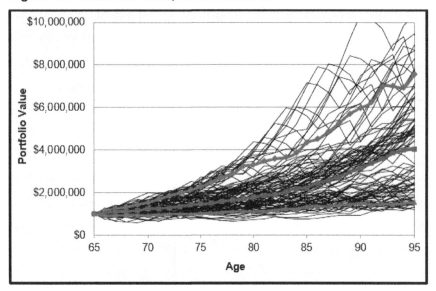

In scenarios like this one, when the withdrawal rate is well below sustainable, then we have effectively an accumulation portfolio. As such, there is no concern for minimum portfolio life. There is no luck factor for Jane because she will have a lifelong income. Here, the luck factor is transferred to Jane's heirs: if they are lucky, they might inherit about $7 million. On the other hand, if they are unlucky, they might end up with only $1 million. It will all depend on what kind of secular trend(s) Jane's portfolio will ride during her retirement.

Can asset allocation improve the outcome in this case? The answer is "yes". When the impact of the sequence of returns and inflation is negligible, as is the case here, then asset allocation becomes important. For accumulation portfolios, we optimize the asset mix to seek the highest median portfolio value.

Results for Jane are provided in Table 5, which shows that the value of the median portfolio peaked when the asset mix was at 70% in equities and 30% in fixed income.

In a scenario like this, where the withdrawal rate is well below sustainable, there is no need to allocate any of the retirement assets to guaranteed income. However, before finalizing this plan, there is one last thing to do: run a series of stress tests to make sure the portfolio can withstand unexpected, person-specific events (see page 22). Only after that, you can conclude that Jane's assets will likely provide her with the lifelong retirement income that she expects.

Table 5: Jane's optimum asset allocation

Asset Mix (Equity/ Fixed Income)	Median Portfolio Value ($ million, at age 95)	
0 / 100	$2.31	
30 / 70	$2.68	
40 / 60	$3.29	
50 / 50	$4.05	
60 / 40	$4.32	
70 / 30	$4.52	← maximum
100 / 0	$4.27	

6.3   The Two Dimensions of Income Planning

In any retirement forecast or aftcast chart, there are two dimensions. The first one is the vertical axis. It shows the portfolio value, that is, the dollar dimension. The second one is the horizontal axis. It shows the time dimension, your age. Figure 18 depicts the two dimensions of lifelong income planning in a graphic format.

Figure 18: Impact of Asset Allocation on a distribution portfolio

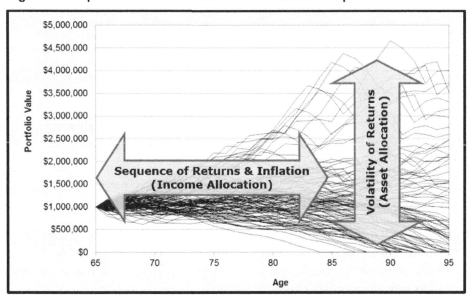

The asset allocation impacts the vertical axis; it controls the *volatility of returns*, the dollar amount of the portfolio value. It is an essential tool for portfolio construction because it generally keeps the dollar amount of portfolio fluctuations within your risk tolerance. This applies to both accumulation as well as all distribution portfolios.

However, asset allocation has little impact on the *sequence of returns*, the portfolio's longevity. In a distribution portfolio, the sequence of returns has much more impact on the portfolio longevity than the volatility of returns. Once the initial withdrawal rate exceeds 3%, then asset allocation alone is insufficient to solve this problem. In these instances, you need to find a way of reducing the withdrawal rate to below the sustainable rate or pool the risk through insurance products, or a combination of both. Later, we will go into more detail about how to use these tools effectively.

6.4   Optimum Asset Allocation

In Scenarios B (Bill) and C (Jane), which we looked at earlier, we made asset mix optimizations based on market history. Using the same logic, we generate the following general guidelines for optimum asset allocation for a variety of scenarios, shown in Table 6.

Table 6: Optimum asset allocation for a buy-and-hold strategy

Scenario	Asset Mix	Investment Income
Accumulation portfolio[10]	60% to 65% equity, the remainder in fixed income	Reinvest dividends, interest, and similar income from distributions
Retirement portfolio where withdrawals plus portfolio costs are less than 3% OR where MRD is not essential for retirement expenses	60% equity / 40% fixed income	Add all interest, dividends, and similar income from distributions to the cash balance
All other retirement portfolios	30% to 40% equity, the remainder in fixed income	Add all interest, dividends, and similar income from distributions to the cash balance

Keep in mind, that each scenario will be different depending on your financial situation and preferences. Furthermore, your own risk tolerance overrides these suggested optimums. We will cover that in Chapter 8, "The Math of Loss".

6.5   Conclusion

Asset allocation is important for managing volatility in a portfolio. It can also improve returns when withdrawal rates are below sustainable. However, its benefits are nowhere near where it is purported to be by the financial industry, particularly for distribution portfolios. It is one of the many tools in the advisor's toolbox, no more, no less, no magic.

---

[10]   First, you need to have a separate "emergency" cash account that holds about one year's expenses. The accumulation portfolio mentioned here is for assets beyond this emergency account.

7 The Impact of Geographic Diversification

In this chapter, we will explore the impact of geographic diversification on a retirement portfolio.

Diversification is one of the essential tenets of prudent investing. Dividing a portfolio into different asset classes will minimize the risk. When one segment of a portfolio is not doing well, a different segment might be performing great. Generally, this reduces the volatility and it can also improve returns, which is a great thing for the portfolio.

7.1 Impact on Distribution Portfolios

For distribution portfolios, which is our focus for this book, proper diversification can reduce volatility, which in turn can minimize the impact of reverse-dollar-cost-averaging. That is a good thing.

The basic asset classes are equities, bonds, hedge funds, cash, income-producing real estate, land, gold, natural resources, inflation-indexed bonds, cash, art, collectibles, and so on. Equities are divided into company size (large-cap, mid-cap, small-cap), or style (growth, value). They can also be divided based on their geography: domestic, U.S., emerging, developed, Latin America, BRIC, and so on.

Earlier, we looked at the market behavior in the random and extreme regions of the probability curve. This behavior applies to geographic diversification in a specific way. When markets are in a random region, geographic diversification works well. However, when a specific stock market in one geographic region moves from random to the left extreme, bad losses can become contagious. The correlation between different geographic regions rapidly increases and the correlation coefficient moves towards one. That means a greatly diminished benefit of diversification in times of crisis.

7.2 Geographic Diversification Scenarios

Let us study the impact of geographic diversification by looking at four different geographic scenarios. The following is common to all scenarios:

- each person is 65 years old and retiring now;
- income is required until age 96;
- retirement savings are valued at $1 million;
- asset mix: as stated in each scenario, rebalanced annually;
- on the equity side, the average annual dividend is 2%;
- on the fixed income side, the return is 0.5% over and above the 6-month CD rate after all costs, using US history;
- we ignore the exchange rate fluctuations between currencies; and
- the annual withdrawals are $60,000, indexed to inflation.

What is not common is that each scenario has a different geographic equity mix, which we cover in each of the four scenarios below.

7.2.1 Scenario A – The United States

Steve lives in the U.S.A. We used four different mixes to see the impact of diversification:

- 100% DJIA (which has 30 stocks in the index);
- 100% S&P500 (500 stocks in this index);
- 30% S&P500, 10% Nikkei225, 60% fixed income;
- 25% S&P500, 8% Nikkei225, 4% FTSE, 3% SP/TSX, 60% fixed income.

Table 7 shows the shortest portfolio life; the age the portfolio depletes for each equity mix.

Table 7: Scenario A – Shortest Portfolio Life for Steve

Equity Proxy	Shortest Portfolio Life (age when portfolio depleted)
100% DJIA	80
100% S&P500	79
30% S&P500, 10% Nikkei225	80
25% S&P500, 8% Nikkei225, 4% FTSE, 3% SP/TSX	80

Figure 19 shows the aftcast when 100% S&P500 is used as the equity proxy. If Steve was the unluckiest retiree, his portfolio would have depleted at age 79.

Figure 19: Aftcast for Steve

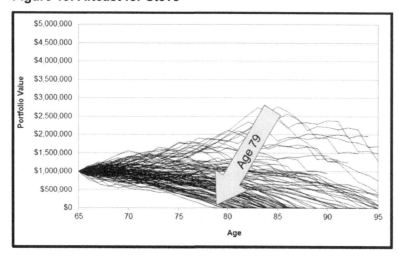

7.2.2 Scenario B – Canada

Cathy lives in Canada. Here, we used two different mixes.

Table 8 shows the shortest portfolio life for each asset mix. Figure 20 shows the aftcast when 100% SP/TSX is used as the equity proxy. The portfolio of the unluckiest retiree would have depleted at age 79.

Table 8: Scenario B – Shortest Portfolio Life for Cathy

Equity Proxy	Shortest Portfolio Life (age when portfolio depleted)
100% SP/TSX	79
25% SP/TSX, 8% S&P500, 3% FTSE, 4% Nikkei225	80

Figure 20: Aftcast for Cathy

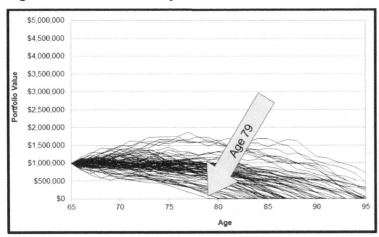

7.2.3 Scenario C – Japan

Yoshie lives in Japan. We used two different mixes.

Table 9 shows the shortest portfolio life, while Figure 21 shows the aftcast when 100% Nikkei225 is used as the equity proxy. The portfolio of the unluckiest retiree would have depleted at age 79.

Table 9: Scenario C – Shortest Portfolio Life for Yoshie

Equity Proxy	Shortest Portfolio Life (age when portfolio depleted)
100% Nikkei225	79
25% Nikkei225, 8%S&P500, 3% FTSE, 4% SP/TSX	81

Figure 21: Aftcast for Yoshie

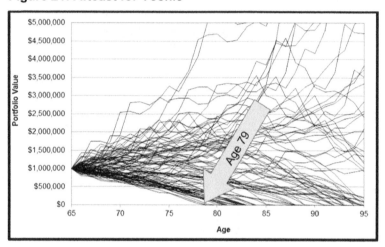

7.2.4 Scenario D – United Kingdom

Charles lives in the United Kingdom. We used two different mixes to see the impact of portfolio diversification.

Table 10 shows the shortest portfolio life, while Figure 22 shows the aftcast when 100% FTSE is used as the equity proxy. The portfolio of the unluckiest retiree would have depleted at age 79, the same age as all other three geographies.

Table 10: Scenario D – Shortest Portfolio Life for Charles

Equity Proxy	Shortest Portfolio Life (age when portfolio depleted)
100% FTSE	79
25% FTSE, 8% S&P500, 4% Nikkei225, 3% SP/TSX	80

Figure 22: Aftcast for Charles

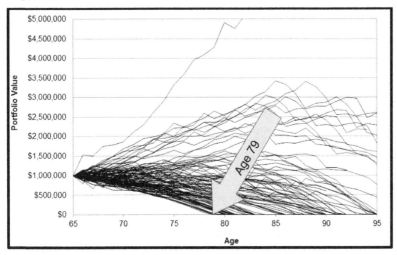

7.3 Conclusion

Diversification is an important tool in portfolio construction. It can reduce volatility and improve returns.

However, do not overestimate its benefits. Especially when the withdrawal rate is larger than the sustainable rate, geographic diversity has little impact on portfolio longevity. In these cases, geographic diversification is not too useful.

8 The Math of Loss

In this chapter, we will look into how losses impact a retirement portfolio. We will cover three areas:

- the gain required to breakeven after a loss;
- the probability of breaking even after a loss;
- time it takes to recover from a loss; and
- the tolerable asset allocation.

8.1 Gain Required to Break Even

For an accumulation portfolio, the mathematics of loss is a simple calculation: If you paid $10 per share last week and it is now $8, you lost $2. The loss is 20%, based on the original share price of $10. To go back to the break-even point, you have to make $2, which is 25% of the current share price of $8.

Table 11 shows how much you need to gain to break even after a loss.

Table 11: Gain required to break even after a loss, accumulation portfolio

% Loss	Total % Gain required to break even
10%	11.1%
20%	25.0%
30%	42.9%
50%	100.0%

Note that there is no time dimension in this table. For example, if you lose 20%, then you need a 25% gain to break even, whether it happens the next day or the next year.

On the other hand, when we talk about distribution portfolios, each withdrawal after a loss creates an additional permanent loss. Not only you do need to recover from the initial loss, but you also need to recover from these seemingly small chunks of permanent loss created along the way. Therefore, Table 11 does not apply to distribution portfolios. We need to attach a time dimension to calculate the total gain required after a loss in a distribution portfolio.

A typical cyclical trend has usually a 3-year recovery time period after a loss. So, we consider a 3–year recovery time for our calculations. Furthermore, we apply a 2% annual indexation of withdrawals. Table 12 shows how much total gain is required after a loss for different withdrawal rates, assuming a steady increase in the portfolio value after the initial loss.

Table 12: Gain required to break even after a loss, distribution portfolio

% Loss	Total % Gain required to break even within 3 years		
	Initial Withdrawal Rate: **2%**	Initial Withdrawal Rate: **4%**	Initial Withdrawal Rate: **6%**
10%	18.3%	25.8%	33.6%
20%	33.4%	42.3%	51.5%
30%	53.0%	63.6%	74.7%
50%	116.1%	133.2%	151.3%

It is interesting to note that, after a 20% loss in an accumulation portfolio, you need a 25% gain to break even (see Table 11). On the other hand, if you want to stick to the same 25% gain hurdle while withdrawing 4%, then you can afford to lose only about 10%, that is, only half as much of the accumulation portfolio as we see in Table 12.

If you are transitioning from accumulation to retirement, this finding suggests that you should consider designing your retirement portfolio with half of the volatility of your accumulation portfolio. Doing so will generate a loss-recovery experience of similar magnitude, before and after retirement. Several years after retirement (at least 5 years), if your portfolio remains in the green zone, you can then consider migrating to a higher-risk asset mix if you want.

8.2 Probability to Break Even

You might be wondering what the historical probability of breakeven after a loss. For that, we start with a portfolio that has an asset mix of 40% S&P500 and 60% fixed income, rebalanced annually. Table 13 shows the probability of breakeven within three years after a loss for various initial withdrawal rates. Table 14 shows the same for a 10-year recovery time horizon.

Table 13: Historical probability of breakeven after 3 years

% Loss	Historical Probability of Breakeven after a Loss after 3 years			
	No Withdrawals	Initial Withdrawal Rate: **2%**	Initial Withdrawal Rate: **4%**	Initial Withdrawal Rate: **6%**
10%	74%	50%	38%	19%
20%	38%	19%	5%	1%
30%	4%	1%	0%	0%
50%	0%	0%	0%	0%

Table 14: Historical probability of breakeven after 10 years

% Loss	Historical Probability of Breakeven after a Loss after 10 years			
	No Withdrawals	Initial Withdrawal Rate: 2%	Initial Withdrawal Rate: 4%	Initial Withdrawal Rate: 6%
10%	97%	81%	47%	20%
20%	92%	61%	27%	5%
30%	78%	40%	12%	0%
50%	30%	3%	0%	0%

8.3   The Time it Takes to Recover from a Loss

After a significant portfolio loss, we may want to how long it will take to recover. In this section, we try to answer this question. We ran a multitude of scenarios and summarized the results in a single chart in Figure 23.

Let's look at an example: Jeff has a balanced portfolio of $1 million. He does not add any money to it, nor does he need any income from it. So, the accumulation rate[11] is 0%. After an unfortunate market event, his portfolio is down 22%. When can Jeff expect to see his portfolio back at the $1 million mark?

In Figure 23, draw a vertical line (the dashed line on the chart) starting at the 22% initial portfolio loss on the horizontal axis. Continue this line until it reaches the 0% accumulation curve. From this point, draw a horizontal line towards the left axis and read the number: about 4.2 years. This is historically how long it took the median portfolio to reach its pre-loss value.

---

[11] Accumulation rate is the dollar amount of annual additions to the portfolio expressed as a percentage of the dollar amount of the current portfolio value.

Figure 23: Estimating the time it takes to reach the pre-loss median portfolio value

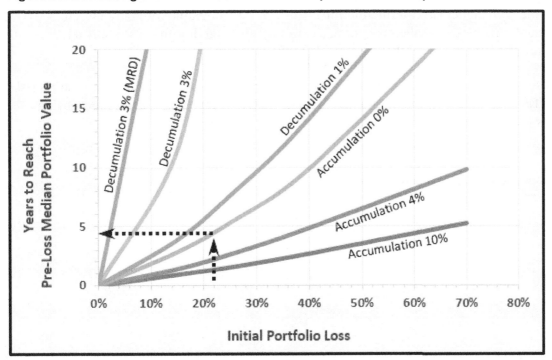

Now, you might wonder what if this loss comes with a "V" shaped recovery (lucky) or a multi-year downturn (unlucky). If you want an accurate answer, then you need to run an aftcast for each specific scenario. However, here is a simple rule of thumb: To estimate the lucky outcome, divide the median by 3. To estimate the unlucky outcome, multiply the median by 2.5. This should cover the vast majority of scenarios.

In our example, the median was 4.2 years. If Jeff is lucky, he will see his portfolio back to $1 million in 1.4 years, calculated as 4.2 divided by 3. On the other hand, if he is unlucky, that day may not come until after 10.5 years, calculated as 4.2 multiplied by 2.5. This assumes that Jeff stays invested throughout and does not bail out.

What about the impact of asset mix? When fractal events happen, asset mix has a large impact on the size of the loss but not as much impact on the recovery time. If the portfolio is heavy in equities, then it loses more, but it also can recover faster. The main risk is your staying power, which is easier to manage in a "V" type recovery.

In Figure 23, we used a 40/60 asset mix for decumulation and 70/30 for accumulation portfolios. If your asset allocation is somewhat different from this, it will still give you a good approximation, give or take a few months.

8.4 Tolerable Asset Allocation

We covered the optimum asset mix based on the market history in Chapter 6. Here, we will cover the tolerable asset mix, which is the asset mix that limits the volatility to a level that you can tolerate.

Historically, equities outperformed fixed-income investments over the long term. However, equities come with higher short-term volatility. This can be intolerable for many investors. To achieve long–term objectives, the investor needs to stay invested. For that, the short-term volatility must be kept at a level that is tolerable to the investor.

The purpose of tolerable asset allocation is to restrain short-term losses within an investor's risk tolerance. Table 15 shows the maximum historical annual loss for various asset mixes using S&P500 as the equity proxy.

Table 15: Maximum historical annual loss

Asset Mix (Equity / Fixed Income)	Maximum Loss
30 / 70	14%
40 / 60	19%
50 / 50	24%
60 / 40	29%
70 / 30	34%

Example: Paula does not want to see a loss of more than 20% in a year. What is her tolerable asset mix?

Answer: Looking at Table 15, we observe that an asset mix of 40% equity and 60% fixed income should limit the annual loss to 20%.

Keep in mind; that tolerable asset allocation does not limit your *total* loss, but only the *annual* loss. For example; if you select an asset mix that limits the annual loss to 15%, in a multi-year bear market, you can still have another 15% loss in the following year(s). In other words, tolerable asset allocation gives you time and financial resilience to review strategies going forward.

Often, when you are looking at both the optimum asset mix (from Table 6) and the tolerable asset mix (Table 15), one of them will point to a lower equity allocation. In this case, choose the asset mix with the lower equity content (see Figure 24). Otherwise, if you bail out of your investments because of intolerable volatility, then you will end up with larger losses.

Figure 24: Choosing your Optimum Asset Mix

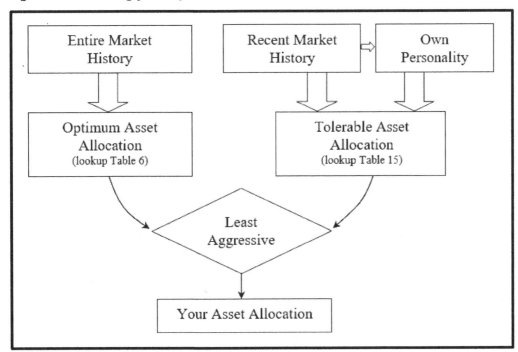

8.5 Examples of Math of Loss

Below are two examples showing the detrimental effect of the math of loss in retirement portfolios.

Example: It is the beginning of 1929. Jack has $1,000,000 of savings in his investment account, invested 100% in DJIA, a total return which includes all dividends, less 2% for all portfolio and management expenses. Jack is thinking that the bull market that started in 1921 will continue for a while longer. He decides he can retire now, at age 65. He is planning to withdraw $50,000 per year, indexed to inflation He prepares a forecast with an annual growth assumption of 6% and inflation of 2%. It shows that Jack will have a lifelong income.

Jack soon realizes that 1929 was a bad year to retire. The value of his investments shrunk sharply during the following four years. By the end of 1932, his investments were worth about $130,000.

...continued on the next page

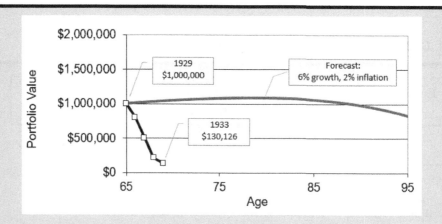

In the summer of 1933, the government introduced a big economic stimulus package. The equity index (plus dividends, minus 2% expenses) went up by 319% until the end of 1936, the largest 4-calendar-year increase in history. Did this help Jack?

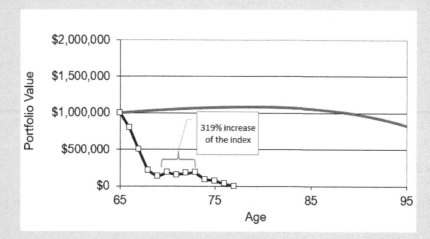

The answer is "not much". This gigantic bullish trend did not do much to recover Jack's portfolio losses. It just gave him a few extra years of income before depleting completely at age 77.

Let's look at a more recent time period.

Example: It is the beginning of 2000. Karen, 65, has $1,000,000 of savings in her investment account, invested 100% in the DJIA; total return includes all dividends less 2% for all portfolio and management expenses. She is thinking that the bull market that started in 1982 will continue. She is retiring now and planning to withdraw $50,000 per year, indexed to inflation. She prepares a forecast with an annual growth assumption of 6% and inflation of 2%. It shows that Karen will have a lifelong income.

Karen soon realizes that 2000 was a bad year to retire. The value of her investments dropped for the following three years. By the end of 2002, her investments were worth about $587,000.

...continued on the next page

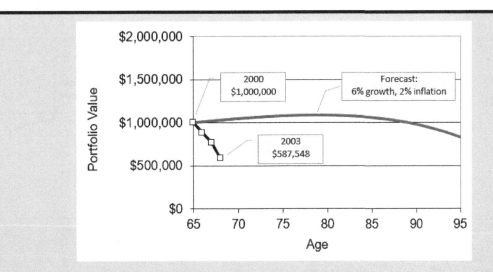

During the five years following 2002, the equity index went up by about 62%: Did this help recover Karen's losses?

The answer is "no", it just bought a little time.

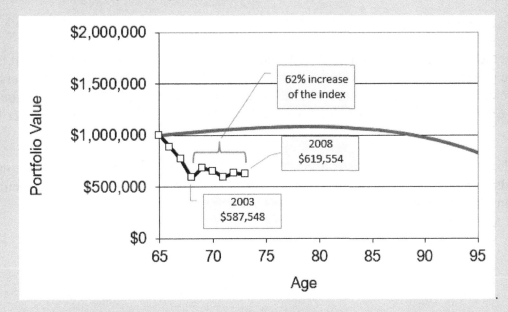

In 2008, the financial crisis hit the markets. Karen's portfolio lost a lot of money. However, since then, markets have been steadily going up and breaking historical records. Between the beginning of 2009 and the end of 2017, the index gained 300%.

Did this help Karen's portfolio?

...continued on the next page

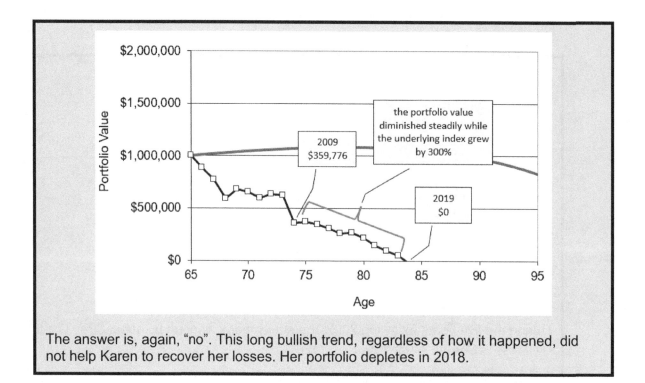

The answer is, again, "no". This long bullish trend, regardless of how it happened, did not help Karen to recover her losses. Her portfolio depletes in 2018.

8.6   Conclusions

The math of loss is different for the distribution stage than the accumulation stage. It is a lot more punitive to a portfolio's performance. Any loss, especially during the early years of retirement, increases the chances of portfolio depletion dramatically. Generally, if you have a loss of 10% or more –even just for one year- it might be nearly impossible to recover from it, ever.

Table 16 shows generalized portfolio behavior in various market trends during different secular trends. In a bearish trend, all portfolios go down in value. In bullish and sideway secular trends, accumulation and distribution portfolios behave differently.

Table 16: Portfolio value versus market trend

Secular Trend Type	Portfolio Value Accumulation Stage	Portfolio Value Distribution Stage Withdrawals less than 4%	Portfolio Value Distribution Stage Withdrawals larger than 4%
Bearish ⬇	Down ⬇	Down ⬇	Down ⬇
Sideways ➡	Flat ➡	Flat ➡	Down ⬇
Bullish ⬆	Up ⬆	Up ⬆	Flat ➡

After the first loss, the die is cast. Once the withdrawal rate exceeds 4% of the portfolio value two years in a row, the asset value of a distribution portfolio disconnects from the underlying markets; it stops going up when the underlying markets go up[12]. On a daily basis, you may see a higher portfolio value after strong days and feel good about it. But at the end of the year, the most you can hope for is a flat portfolio value, even when markets might be soaring. After this point, even the strongest bullish trend cannot save a distribution portfolio from its eventual demise.

It is best not to lose, give away, donate, part with, gift, help out or misplace any retirement savings, especially during the early years of retirement.

---

[12] There is one exception to this: for tax-sheltered portfolios where MRD applies, if this income is not needed and it is reinvested in an open account, then you can treat the combined portfolio as sustainable (on Table 16, column "required withdrawals less than 4%").

9 Warning Signals of Diminishing Luck

How would you know if you are running out of luck? Is there any way of telling that you might be going from being lucky to unlucky?

After the withdrawal rate, the luck factor is the second-largest determinant of a portfolio's longevity. Therefore, it is important to keep an eye out for warning signals that indicate diminishing luck. In this chapter, we will look at three different warning signals that can provide answers:

- Price-Earnings Ratio: A fundamental analysis signal – "Is the market overheated now?"

- Hurricane Warning: A technical analysis signal – "What is the long-term trend?"

- Fifth Year Check-up: A measure combining the bad sequence of returns, excessive inflation, inability to stick to the original retirement plan, etc. – "How did I do during my first five years of retirement?"

9.1 Price-Earnings Ratio

The Price Earnings ratio, otherwise known as the PE ratio, is calculated by dividing the stock price of a company by its earnings. For example, if the stock price for XYZ Inc. is $50, and it earned $4.17 per share in the previous four quarters, then the PE ratio of XYZ Inc. is 12, calculated as $50 / $4.17.

PE ratio is a fundamental analysis tool. It is a measure of the value of a stock against its peers, as well as against the market. In general, it indicates if a company's share price is overpriced, fairly priced, or underpriced.

The average of all PE ratios of all companies in the equity index tells us if the entire market is overpriced, fairly priced, or underpriced. If the average PE ratio of the equity index is high, then it is overvalued. This can be especially risky for a retired person. We cannot predict when a correction will happen, but we don't need to. Sooner or later, the overvalued market undergoes a correction, and this can create a bad sequence of returns. Figure 25 depicts the chain of events that a high PE ratio can trigger.

Figure 25 depicts the chain of events that a high PE ratio can trigger.

Figure 25: Chain of events of a high PE ratio of the equity index

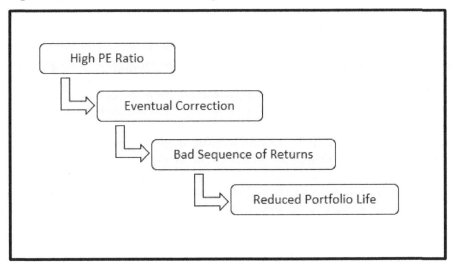

The average market PE ratio can be a good predictor of a portfolio's longevity for portfolios with high withdrawal rates. Figure 26 shows the close relationship between the portfolio life and the average market PE ratio.

Figure 26: Correlation between portfolio life and the PE ratio

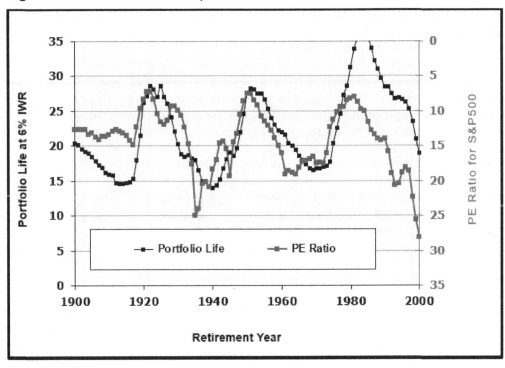

The red line in Figure 26 is the average market PE ratio. Read its value on the vertical axis on the right-hand side of the chart. Note that, for the equity index, we use S&P500 because it has by far the largest impact on the equity markets all around the world.

The black line on the same chart is the portfolio life based on a 6% initial withdrawal rate (IWR) for an asset mix of 40% equity (S&P500) and 60% fixed income, rebalanced annually. Read its value on the vertical axis on the left-hand side of the chart.

We observe that black and red lines generally move up and down together, i.e., they are correlated. A simple analysis reveals the expected life for a well-diversified portfolio when the withdrawal rate is larger than sustainable, can be estimated (to within a couple of years) by the formula:

- For 6% IWR: portfolio life = 4 + (250 / PE)
- For 5% IWR: portfolio life = 4 + (360 / PE)

For other withdrawal rates:

- if the IWR is larger than 6%, you don't need a formula to estimate the portfolio life, it will be short;
- if the IWR is near sustainable (between 3.5% and 4%), the data is too scattered for a reliable formula to estimate the portfolio life; and
- if the IWR is below sustainable, under 3.5%, then you have –in effect- an accumulation portfolio and it should provide lifelong income.

Example: At the end of 1999, the PE ratio for S&P500 was 30. If we assume an initial withdrawal rate of 5%, indexed to inflation, starting at the beginning of 2000, we can estimate the approximate portfolio life as follows:

Portfolio Life for 5% IWR = 4 + (360 / 30) = 16 years

Compare this with the portfolio life observed in Karen's example in Chapter 8.4: she retired in 2000 and her portfolio depleted in a little over 18 years. This is close to the estimated portfolio life using the formula above.

Rule of thumb: If one retires when the average market PE ratio is higher than 12 and the withdrawal rate is larger than 4%, then any forecast that is based on the average growth rate and average inflation will be far too optimistic.

9.2 Hurricane Warning

The hurricane warning is a technical analysis tool. It shows the long-term trend of the market. It uses moving averages to give you a warning about a pending risk of a bad sequence of returns. Here is how it works:

- Using a monthly chart for S&P500, draw 5-month and 12-month simple moving averages. You can do so easily on many websites[13].

- If the 5–month moving average moves below the 12–month moving average and the 12–month moving average is declining, then markets may be going into a bearish trend. Go defensive.

- Otherwise, stay the course.

Do not expect to catch the exact market top or market bottom. Also, keep in mind, that you will get false warning signals.

Figure 27 depicts the hurricane warning signals that were generated over the last twenty years. Red arrows pointing down indicate the start of the hurricane warning and green arrows pointing up indicate the end of it.

Figure 27: Hurricane warning signals

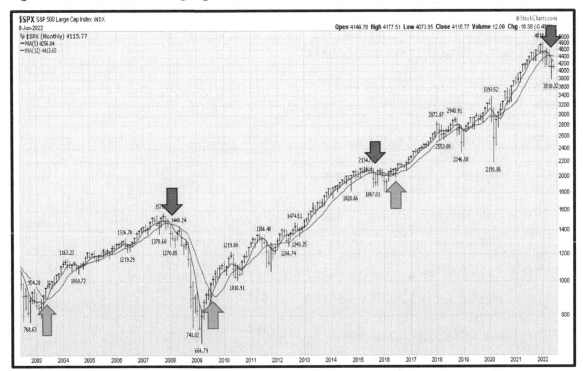

---

[13] www.stockcharts.com

9.3   Fifth Year Check-up

A lot of things happen during the first five years of retirement. Our foremost concern is the sustainability of life-long income. Its strongest antagonist is a bad sequence of returns. But it is not the only one. There are others: high inflation, asset mix that is too aggressive (or too conservative), the impact of reverse-dollar-cost-averaging, underperforming investments, low-interest rates, withdrawing more than originally planned, and so on.

The fifth-year check-up combines the impact of all these pieces of the jigsaw puzzle into a single picture. It is the chart depicted in Figure 28. It shows how long a portfolio can generate income in the worst-case scenario, based on history.

For the fifth-year check-up, we need five pieces of data:

- The start age of withdrawals. This is usually the start age of retirement, but not always so.
- The initial portfolio value,
- The initial withdrawal amount,
- The current portfolio value after five years of withdrawals, and
- Total withdrawals over the first five years of retirement.

Let's demonstrate this with a worked example.

Example: Jackie retired at age 65 with $ 1 million in her portfolio. She planned to withdraw $35,000 / year. She is now 70, her portfolio is worth $956,000. Over the past 5 years, Jackie withdrew $181,410 in total.

Jackie wants to know until what age she can expect her portfolio to last in the worst case, based on market history.

STEP 1: Calculate Initial Withdrawal Rate: $\frac{Initial\ Withdrawal\ Amount}{Initial\ Portfolio\ Value}$ X 100%

$$IWR = \frac{\$35,000}{\$1,000,000} \times 100\% = 3.5\%$$

STEP 2: Calculate Net Invested: Initial Portfolio Value - Total Withdrawals

Net Invested = $1,000,000 - $181,410 = $818,590

STEP 3: Calculate Net Growth: Current Portfolio Value - Net Invested

Net Growth = $956,000 - $818,410 = $137,410

STEP 4: Calculate Income Coverage: $\frac{Net\ Growth}{Total\ Withdrawals}$ X 100%

Income Coverage $= \frac{\$137,410}{\$181,410} \times 100\% = 76\%$

...continued on the next page

STEP 5: Now look up in graph (Figure 28):

    1) Starting on the horizontal axis, income coverage at 76%, draw a vertical line until it intersects the line that says "IWR: 3.5%".

    2) From this point, draw a horizontal line until it meets the left axis.

    3) Read the year on the left axis, in this case, 30 years.

    4) This is the shortest portfolio life that happened historically.

    5) Now, add this number to the starting age of withdrawals, 65.
        65 + 30 = 95.

Answer: All else being equal, the market history indicates that Jackie's portfolio should survive at least until Jackie is 95.

Keep in mind, that the graph in Figure 28 works only if the net growth over five years (calculated in Step 3 above) is larger than zero. Otherwise, redo the entire plan from scratch as if the retirement is starting right now, and seriously consider including guaranteed income in your plans.

Figure 28: Fifth-year check-up, estimating worst-case portfolio life

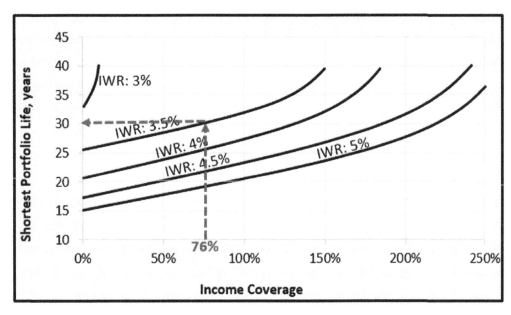

9.4 Conclusion

These three warning signals can give you advance notice of fading luck.

- The PE ratio is checked only once, at the start of retirement. It can give you many years in advance warning.

- The hurricane warning signal is monitored monthly. It requires immediate action. By the time it is visible, a bad sequence of returns is probably already underway. It can protect the portfolio from the worst losses. Yet it can be a false signal, and this can cost some loss of opportunity by being out of the market unnecessarily.

- The fourth-year check-up is done only once. It tells you if you have experienced a bad sequence of returns in the early years of retirement.

If you see any of these warning signals, you need to consider reducing riskier investments in the portfolio and/or buying guaranteed income, such as life annuities.

10 Sustainable Withdrawal Rate

In this chapter, we will discuss the Sustainable Withdrawal Rate (SWR) and how we can use it for retirement income planning.

SWR is the **maximum** amount of money that you can withdraw from a portfolio throughout retirement with an **acceptable** risk of depletion. It is customary to express it in terms of a percentage, such as the famous "4% rule", which suggests that if you start withdrawing the dollar amount that is equal to 4% of your retirement assets at the beginning of retirement, and index this to CPI each year, then you would have income for 30 years at a reasonable risk.

It is important to note that the SWR percentage is used only to calculate the starting withdrawal amount -in dollars- for the first year. After that, the percentage disappears; all you need to do is to index this dollar amount to CPI each year for the rest of the retirement time horizon or until the next income review.

The SWR is based on historic extremes of the past. Future black swan events will be different. Therefore, it is important to review the portfolio sustainability once every five years or after major life events (such as death, or long-term care) and adjust for changing income needs. This is the only time when the SWR *percentage* is looked up again and the sustainable dollar amount is recalculated.

Another important reason for the five-year review is this: the SWR is based on market extremes. It is unlikely that you will have as much damage as the market in a black swan event. Therefore, it is quite probable (and a nice surprise) to see a pay increase after the review.

You might have come across different SWR rates in various financial publications. The reason for this wide range is the inputs used in different studies. Some of the factors that affect the SWR are (not in any order of importance):

- Total return versus index return: the current average dividend yield is half of what it was pre-1990s. If the historic dividend yield is included (also called, the total return) in SWR calculations, you will end up with an overly optimistic SWR going forward. If you see that an SWR is based on total returns, disregard it.

- Man-made MC simulators versus actual historical data: As discussed earlier, MC simulators have significant deficiencies in modeling the market behavior outside the random region. If the SWR figures are generated using MC simulators, you will likely end up with overly optimistic SWRs. For example, if you see that a 100% equity portfolio has a lower probability of depletion than a 50/50 mix for a decumulation portfolio, then the model is flawed, disregard it.

- Asset allocation: this can have some impact on the SWR, but generally a lot less so than generally proclaimed by the financial industry.

- Choice of equity index: There are differences between how various equity indices behave. Generally, a model that is based on a specific index might not work for a broader index.

- Adaptive asset allocation, novel risk management and withdrawal strategies: these can have some impact on the SWR. However, their impact is usually overblown. It is advisable to disregard any SWR numbers based on unproven strategies.
- Portfolio costs: They can have an important impact on SWRs. The higher the portfolio costs, the lower the SWR for the retiree. If a study ignores portfolio costs, disregard it.
- Underperformance: It is demonstrated repeatedly, that most fund managers (and investors) underperform the index over long periods. This is usually because of behavioral factors, the size of assets managed, and the dynamics of money flow. This will make a difference in the SWR analysis.

Here, we use aftcasting which preserves the sequence of returns as well as all correlations between stocks, bonds, interest, and inflation rate, resulting in a much more reliable SWR.

10.1 Acceptable Risk

There is one very important factor, perhaps more important than all of the above, and it is the definition of "acceptable risk". We already know that the SWR is based on a specific degree of **acceptable** risk within a given time horizon. So, we must ask: "What is the acceptable risk?"

How you answer this question makes a big difference. For example; an academic study that allows a 25% failure rate in their SWR tables[14] is not acceptable in real life. When retirement income is at stake, you certainly want a lower level of risk of running out of money.

The simple answer is, that what is acceptable depends on what this money is needed for. Is this money for groceries or is it to help fund your grandchild for her overseas vacation?

We assign each expense item to one of these three categories: Essential, Basic, and Discretionary. Each category has a different acceptable level of risk. So, we generate SWR for each.

- **Essential Expenses:** These are expenses that are necessary for survival. Here, the probability of portfolio depletion must be zero. Generally, housing expenses, income taxes, and most living expenses are in this group.

  Here, our acceptable risk is "the occasional loss of purchasing power must not be larger than 10% at any age". Because the acceptable risk for essential expenses is the lowest of these three groups of expenses, it demands the highest funding factor, that is, it needs the largest amount of assets for each dollar to be withdrawn.

- **Basic Expenses:** These are lifestyle expenses that are not critical for survival. For example, if you love going south each winter, when push comes to shove (financially), you can probably do without it. So, this is a non-essential, but desirable expense.

  Here, our acceptable risk is "the probability of portfolio depletion should not exceed 10%". That means, there is a 10% chance that you might have to forego this category of expenses at some point during retirement.

---

[14] I have seen a few of these over my 25-year experience in the investment business.

- **Discretionary Expenses:** These are expenses such as donations, multiple vacation homes, financial assistance to relatives, etc. If the money is not there, it won't be spent and that will not change your lifestyle (much).

  Here, the acceptable risk is, "the median outcome must last until death", 50% probability of portfolio depletion at death. This category of expenses affords a much larger SWR and therefore, it demands the lowest funding factor.

Figure 29 depicts the correlation between SWR and acceptable risk in a visual format.

Figure 29: SWR versus acceptable risk for different groups of retirement expenses

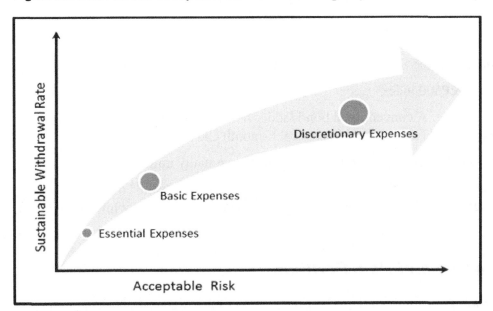

Keep in mind; that only you (not the advisor) decide which expense item is essential, which is basic, and which is discretionary. For example: for family "A", living in the suburbs, two cars can be essential. For family "B", the first car can be essential and the second car, discretionary. For family "C" living in downtown of a big city, both cars might be in the discretionary category.

Another example: helping with a grandchild's expenses can be a discretionary expense, but helping with a *disabled* grandchild's expenses can be essential.

Ultimately, it is your decision as to which category to assign an expense item to. Also, do not tack on excessive contingency for expenses to your base case, they should only be added later as part of the stress test scenarios.

The initial discovery process for expense items can be a time-consuming exercise. However, once you establish this baseline, future reviews become much easier.

10.2 Income from Other Sources

The next item in the discovery process is a review of expected income from all other sources. This list should include income from government retirement benefits (social security), company pensions, annuity income, rental income, business income, royalties, and so on. Do not include income from investments (open or tax-sheltered) because they are calculated separately based on the SWR.

We will later see that, to finance each dollar of retirement expense for life, you will require as much as $34 in retirement savings. Therefore, it is important to prepare the income and expense projections as thoroughly as possible.

10.3 Assumptions for SWR Calculations

Here are the assumptions for the SWR calculations in this chapter:

- Equity: S&P500 index

- Fixed income: A conventional bond ladder held until maturity, no capital gains or losses, net yield after costs is historical 6-month CD plus 1%.

- Withdrawal amount: indexed to historical CPI annually until death.

- Longevity Risk: all SWR tables are based on the age of death[15] of 96. This provides about a 90% certainty your portfolio does not deplete while you are still alive.

10.4 SWR for a Buy-and-Hold Portfolio

For the SWR calculation for a "buy-and-hold" portfolio, we use an asset mix is 40% equities, and 60% fixed income/cash. This allocation is kept constant for the entire retirement time horizon. It is rebalanced annually. Keeping in mind that each expense type has a different level of acceptable risk, the SWRs for each expense group is provided in Table 17.

Table 17: SWR for a buy-and-hold portfolio, age of death 96

Retirement Age	Sustainable Withdrawal Rate		
	for Essential Expenses	for Basic Expenses	for Discretionary Expenses
60	2.85%	3.48%	4.20%
65	3.10%	3.83%	4.65%
70	3.46%	4.34%	5.33%
75	4.01%	5.01%	6.39%
80	5.05%	6.22%	8.44%

---

[15] Age 96 is a default for these tables. We will show later how to look up SWR for different time horizons.

10.5 Using the SWR to Determine if You Have Enough

We can use these SWRs to determine if you have enough assets for life.

> **Example:** Robert, 70, is just retiring. He has $600,000 in his retirement portfolio. After taking into account his social security benefits, he still needs some more for his essential expenses. How much more income can he take out from his portfolio?
>
> Looking up Table 17, at age 70, the SWR for essential expenses is 3.46%. Robert can withdraw up to $20,760 each year from his portfolio for his essential expenses, calculated as $600,000 x 0.0346

The SWR tells us how much we can withdraw from retirement assets. If the question is "Do I have sufficient assets for lifelong expenses?" then divide the expenses required by the SWR for each type of expense.

> **Continuing with the previous example:**
>
> For his essential expenses, Robert figures that he needs $5,000 per year from his savings, in addition to social security benefits. He also needs $15,000 per year for his basic expenses and $4,000 per year for his discretionary expenses. Does he have enough savings?
>
> Essential Expenses: Divide $5,000 by the SWR for essential expenses, 3.46%, to calculate to cover his essential expenses: $5,000 / 0.0346 = $144,509. Robert needs $144,509 of retirement assets to generate $5,000 per year of essential expenses (indexed to CPI for the rest of his life).
>
> Basic Expenses: The SWR for basic expenses: at age 70 is 4.34%. Divide $15,000 by 4.34% to calculate the assets required for his basic expenses: $15,000 / 0.0434 = $345,622
>
> Discretionary Expenses: The SWR for discretionary expenses: at age 70 is 5.33%. Divide $4,000 by 5.33% to calculate how much assets he needs for his discretionary expenses: $4,000 / 0.0533 = $75,047
>
> Total assets required to cover all expenses is: $144,509 + $345,622 + 75,047 = $565,178. Robert has $600,000, enough savings to cover everything.

10.5.1 Different Ages of Death

The SWR tables assume a retirement time horizon until age 96. Can you calculate for a different age of death? Yes, you can. Here is the same example of using the age of death as 101:

Continuing with the previous example:

Considering his family history, Robert wants to plan his retirement income until age 101, not 96. Recalculate the adequacy of his retirement assets based on this requirement.

The SWR table (Table 17) is based on the age of death of 96. To use the SWR table for an additional 5 years of time horizon, just look up the SWR for age 65, even though Robert is 70 years old right now. This will give the SWR needed for the additional five years of longevity.

Essential expenses: SWR at age 65 is 3.10%. Assets required for essential expenses: $5,000 / 0.0310 = $161,290

Basic Expenses: The SWR for basic expenses: at age 65 is 3.83%. Assets required for basic expenses: $15,000 / 0.0383 = $391,645

Assets left for discretionary expenses:
$600,000 - $161,290 - $391,645 = $47,065

Discretionary Expenses: The SWR for discretionary expenses: at age 65 is 4.65%. Assets required for discretionary expenses: $4,000 / 0.0465 = $86,022

He has only $47,065 left for his discretionary expenses, but he needs to have $86,022 for this.

If Robert were to live until age 101, he would have sufficient savings for essential and basic expenses, but not for discretionary expenses. So, he might have to consider reducing his discretionary expenses as he gets older.

10.5.2 If Other Income Sources Cover Essential Expenses

Some retirees have significant amounts of guaranteed income from government and employer pensions, which cover all their essential expenses. The following example shows how to calculate the savings required for basic and discretionary expenses.

Example: Jack and Nancy are both 65, just retiring. They have combined retirement assets of $1.2 million. Their combined government benefits are $36,000 per year. In addition, Nancy has an indexed pension that pays $22,000 per year.

Their annual expenses are $95,000 per year, of which $45,000 is for essential expenses, $40,000 is for basic expenses, and $10,000 is for discretionary expenses. Do they have sufficient assets to finance their retirement expenses?

Essential Expenses: Their income from other sources add up to $58,000 (calculated as $36,000 plus $22,000). Their essential expenses are $45,000. Income from other sources pays their essential expenses in full, and there is a surplus of $13,000 that we carry over towards meeting their basic expenses (calculated as $58,000 less $45,000). Jack and Nancy don't need any savings to meet their essential expenses.

Basic Expenses: Their basic expenses are $40,000. We carried over the surplus of $13,000 from income from other sources. This means they need to withdraw $27,000 from their retirement assets (calculated as $40,000 - $13,000) to cover their basic expenses.

The SWR for basic expenses: at age 65 is 3.83%. Divide $27,000 by 3.83% to calculate how much assets they need for their basic expenses: $27,000 / 0.0383 = $704,961

They have sufficient savings to cover their basic expenses. Now, they have $495,039 left for discretionary expenses (calculated as $1.2 million less $704,961)

Discretionary Expenses: Their discretionary expenses are $10,000 per year. The SWR for discretionary expenses: at age 65 is 4.65%. Divide $10,000 by 4.65% to calculate how much assets they need for discretionary expenses $10,000 / 0.0465 = $215,054

They have sufficient savings to cover all their retirement expenses, including their discretionary expenses.

10.6 Stress Testing Assets

The SWR figures are based on historical market performance. What if the future performance is less favorable than it was in the past?

We calculate the SWR figures with the following stress-test assumptions:

- Equities underperform the index by 1%
- Fixed Income: net yield 0.5% lower than in the base case
- Inflation rate is on average 0.5% higher than in the base case.

The resulting SWR is presented in Table 18. Keep in mind; that these figures are only used for stress testing purposes and only after determining that you have already sufficient assets to cover retirement expenses. If a retirement portfolio is insufficient to start with, stress testing has no meaning.

Table 18: SWR for a buy-and-hold portfolio for stress testing purpose

Retirement Age	Sustainable Withdrawal Rate		
	for Essential Expenses	for Basic Expenses	for Discretionary Expenses
60	2.36%	2.91%	3.52%
65	2.63%	3.29%	3.98%
70	2.99%	3.79%	4.63%
75	3.55%	4.49%	5.65%
80	4.58%	5.72%	7.81%

Here is a stress-test example, using the same scenario above, of Jack and Nancy.

Continuing with the previous example:

Jack and Nancy want to stress-test their portfolio for adverse portfolio performance. They also want to see the adequacy of their retirement assets if their essential expenses were $50,000 ($5,000 per year higher) and their basic expenses are $43,000 ($3,000 per year higher). Their discretionary expenses remain the same as before, $10,000 per year.

Essential Expenses: Their income from other sources is $58,000. Their essential expenses are $50,000. So, income from other sources pays their essential expenses in full, and there is a surplus of $8,000 which we carry over to basic expenses (calculated as $58,000 less $50,000). Jack and Nancy don't need any savings to meet their essential expenses.

Basic Expenses: Their basic expenses are $43,000 per year. We carried over a surplus of $8,000 from other income after paying their essential expenses. This means they need to withdraw $35,000 from their retirement assets (calculated as $43,000 -$8,000) to cover their basic expenses.

The SWR (for stress testing purposes) for basic expenses: at age 65 is 3.29% (from Table 18). Divide $35,000 by 3.29% to calculate how much assets they need for their basic expenses: $35,000 / 0.0329 = $1,063,830

They have sufficient savings to cover their basic expenses. Now, they have $136,170 left for discretionary expenses (calculated as $1.2 million less $1,063,830)

Discretionary Expenses: Their discretionary expenses are $10,000 per year. The SWR (for stress testing purposes) for discretionary expenses: at age 65 is 3.98%. Divide $10,000 by 3.98% to calculate how much assets they need for discretionary expenses $10,000 / 0.0398 = $251,256. However, they have left only $136,170 for discretionary expenses. Therefore, if stress conditions occur, they will need to reduce their discretionary expenses to $5,420 per year (calculated as $10,000 x $136,170 / $251,256)

In the final analysis, under these stress test conditions, they have sufficient retirement savings for essential and basic expenses. They do not have sufficient savings for their discretionary expenses. In the future, they might have to decrease their discretionary expenses, if stress test conditions occur.

10.7 Age-based Asset Allocation

According to this strategy, your age, expressed as a percentage, is allocated to fixed income. The remaining assets (100 minus age, expressed as a percentage), are allocated to equities. For example, at age 65, the asset mix is 35% equity and 65% fixed income. At age 75, it is 25% equity and 75% to fixed income. With this strategy, as you get older, the portfolio becomes more conservative. Table 19 shows the SWRs if an age-based asset allocation strategy is used.

Table 19: SWR for age-based asset allocation strategy

Retirement Age	Sustainable Withdrawal Rate		
	for Essential Expenses	for Basic Expenses	for Discretionary Expenses
60	2.64%	3.36%	4.22%
65	2.88%	3.77%	4.72%
70	3.26%	4.45%	5.49%
75	3.92%	5.05%	6.64%
80	5.14%	6.48%	8.54%

Age-based asset allocation strategy generally provides a lower SWR than a buy-and-hold strategy. The reason for that is, that as you get older, equities make up a smaller portion of the portfolio, and that diminishes the opportunity to fight the impact of inflation in the later years. Table 20 shows the SWR for stress testing purposes.

Table 20: SWR for age-based asset allocation strategy for stress testing purpose

Retirement Age	Sustainable Withdrawal Rate		
	for Essential Expenses	for Basic Expenses	for Discretionary Expenses
60	2.19%	2.80%	3.57%
65	2.44%	3.17%	4.07%
70	2.82%	3.92%	4.82%
75	3.48%	4.55%	5.99%
80	4.71%	5.99%	7.94%

10.8 Buy-and-Hold with Asset Dedication

This is the same as the buy-and-hold strategy with one exception: The fixed income (cash and bonds) portion of the portfolio can never hold less than 5 years of withdrawals. If the portfolio value is less than 5 years of withdrawals, then it holds only fixed income and no equities. This strategy can give some comfort with reduced volatility towards the end of life. Table 21 shows the SWRs for this strategy, while Table 22 shows the SWRs for stress testing purposes.

Table 21: SWR for buy-and-hold with asset dedication

Retirement Age	Sustainable Withdrawal Rate		
	for Essential Expenses	for Basic Expenses	for Discretionary Expenses
60	2.86%	3.49%	4.23%
65	3.08%	3.85%	4.64%
70	3.36%	4.28%	5.29%
75	3.83%	4.84%	6.46%
80	4.90%	6.14%	8.35%

Table 22: SWR for buy-and-hold with asset dedication for stress testing purpose

Retirement Age	Sustainable Withdrawal Rate		
	for Essential Expenses	for Basic Expenses	for Discretionary Expenses
60	2.38%	2.91%	3.54%
65	2.61%	3.27%	3.97%
70	2.91%	3.70%	4.66%
75	3.39%	4.32%	5.74%
80	4.44%	5.67%	7.74%

10.9 Bucket Strategy

The bucket strategy involves dividing retirement savings equally into separate "asset buckets". The first bucket pays retirement expenses in the early years of retirement. This bucket usually holds only cash and short-term bonds.

The second bucket holds more aggressive investments than the first one, usually a balanced portfolio. This bucket has more time to grow when withdrawals are from the first bucket. When the first bucket depletes, then the second bucket starts paying retirement expenses.

If more buckets are used, then the third and fourth buckets have increasingly higher equity content.

We analyzed the following bucket strategies:

- Two buckets: Bucket #1: 1/2 of assets, all in fixed income
  Bucket #2: 1/2 of assets, 60% equity, 40% fixed income

- Three Buckets: Bucket #1: 1/3 of assets, all in fixed income
  Bucket #2: 1/3 of assets, 40% equity, 60% fixed income
  Bucket #3: 1/3 of assets, 60% equity, 40% fixed income

- Four Buckets: Bucket #1: 1/4 of assets, all in fixed income
  Bucket #2: 1/4 of assets, 30% equity, 70% fixed income
  Bucket #3: 1/4 of assets, 50% equity, 50% fixed income
  Bucket #4: 1/4 of assets, 70% equity, 30% fixed income

Table 23 shows SWR for the 2-bucket strategy. We did not show here tables for the 3-bucket and 4-bucket strategies, because SWRs for them were nearly identical to the 2-bucket strategy. So, if you have more than two buckets, you can use the same table (Table 23). Keep in mind, that the more buckets you have, the closer you get to a buy-and-hold portfolio. Table 24 shows the SWR for stress testing purposes.

Table 23: SWR for two-bucket strategy

Retirement Age	Sustainable Withdrawal Rate		
	for Essential Expenses	for Basic Expenses	for Discretionary Expenses
60	3.15%	3.61%	4.09%
65	3.44%	3.93%	4.61%
70	3.80%	4.44%	5.30%
75	4.35%	5.13%	6.27%
80	5.39%	6.31%	8.15%

Table 24: SWR for a two-bucket strategy for stress testing purpose

Retirement Age	Sustainable Withdrawal Rate		
	for Essential Expenses	for Basic Expenses	for Discretionary Expenses
60	2.59%	2.97%	3.50%
65	2.90%	3.39%	3.93%
70	3.29%	3.91%	4.55%
75	3.85%	4.60%	5.64%
80	4.87%	5.86%	7.50%

10.10 Growth Harvesting

This is identical to a buy-and-hold strategy with two exceptions:

- The growth of the equity portion of the portfolio is reviewed at the end of each year. If it has grown by more than 8%, we then take 50% of that growth and place it into a separate cash bucket for future retirement income. The target asset mix and rebalancing apply only to the remaining portfolio, excluding the cash bucket; and

- With the buy-and-hold strategy, we had a 40/60 asset mix of equities and fixed income. With growth harvesting, we need more growth initially which we can harvest from. Therefore, the initial asset mix is a bit more aggressive; it is 50/50.

As time goes on, the proportion of the cash bucket grows and the equity portion shrinks in combined assets. Figure 30 depicts a typical, average asset mix over time for the growth harvesting strategy. Table 25 shows the SWRs for the growth harvesting strategy. Table 26 shows the SWR for stress testing purposes.

Figure 30: Typical average asset mix over the retirement time horizon for the growth harvesting strategy

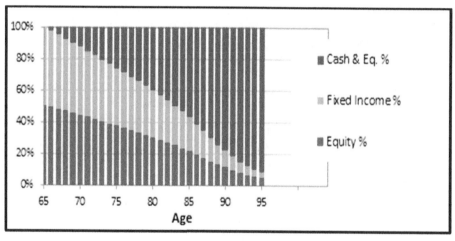

Table 25: SWR for growth harvesting strategy

Retirement Age	Sustainable Withdrawal Rate		
	for Essential Expenses	for Basic Expenses	for Discretionary Expenses
60	2.54%	3.40%	4.30%
65	2.78%	3.79%	4.87%
70	3.14%	4.39%	5.92%
75	3.69%	5.32%	7.76%
80	4.75%	7.19%	10.50%

Table 26: SWR for growth harvesting strategy for stress testing purpose

Retirement Age	Sustainable Withdrawal Rate		
	for Essential Expenses	for Basic Expenses	for Discretionary Expenses
60	2.15%	2.92%	3.72%
65	2.39%	3.29%	4.31%
70	2.74%	3.87%	5.30%
75	3.28%	4.82%	7.06%
80	4.31%	6.74%	9.84%

10.11 The SWR and Life Annuities

A life annuity is a contract between the insurance company and the owner of the annuity. The owner of the annuity (usually the same as the annuitant but not always), hands over a lump sum of money to the insurance company. In return, the insurer promises to pay an income (usually monthly), guaranteed for life, to the annuitant(s).

For risk management, annuities have many advantages over investment portfolios. The first important benefit is the guaranteed income for life, which a regular investment portfolio does not provide. Regardless of how diligently you plan an investment portfolio, income from it is vulnerable to market and longevity risks. On the other hand, with life annuities, once you sign the contract, you know exactly how much it will pay you for life. Market risk, longevity risk, and (to some extent), inflation risk are removed from the scene. You never have to worry about running out of income and you never have to worry about how the market is doing.

The second advantage is, that the payout from a life annuity is always higher than the SWR for essential and basic expenses. There are two reasons for this.

1. The SWR from an investment portfolio must be based on long time horizons to make sure that the portfolio is not depleted prior to death. We used age 96 in our tables above, and we also did a stress test example (Jack and Nancy) using age 101. Insurance companies do not worry about how long an individual lives, they only need to know the average age of the pool of annuitants, which is usually not much higher than the average life expectancy. So, the time horizon of payments that an insurance company uses is probably ten years shorter than the time horizon that we used for our SWR tables. This creates the "age credit" for surviving annuitants; meaning that a surplus of assets left from those who die before life expectancy continues paying the surviving annuitants within the pool; hence a higher annuity payout.

2. Our SWRs for essential expenses are based on the worst-case historic performance. This is to mitigate the luck factor (sequence of returns, inflation, and reverse dollar-cost averaging). On the other hand, because annuities are pooled money, they don't need to take this into account; they just vary the annuity payout rate to reflect the prevailing investment conditions for new purchasers of annuities. The luck factor for the pool is constantly monitored and managed by the insurance company.

Table 27 shows a comparison of buy-and-hold SWR for essential and basic expenses and life annuity[16] payouts.

Table 27: SWR for a buy-and-hold portfolio and payout for life annuity

| Retirement Age | Investment Portfolio | | Life Annuity | |
	SWR for Essential Expenses	SWR for Basic Expenses	Life Annuity Payout, (male)	Life Annuity Payout (female)
60	2.85%	3.48%	3.61%	3.39%
65	3.10%	3.83%	4.38%	4.07%
70	3.46%	4.34%	5.14%	4.82%
75	4.01%	5.01%	6.01%	5.70%
80	5.05%	6.22%	6.88%	6.73%

Another benefit of annuities is, that there is no need to run a stress test. The payment is guaranteed regardless of longevity, market conditions, or performance. In the cash flow list, it is just treated as income from other sources, not subject to SWR calculations.

Figure 31 depicts visually the SWRs versus life annuity payouts. The current life annuity payouts, even in the current low-interest environment, are significantly higher than the SWRs for essential expenses and slightly higher than the SWR for basic expenses.

Figure 31: SWR and life annuity versus acceptable risk

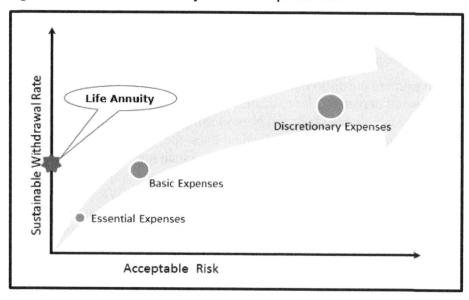

---

[16] Source: estimation based on Cannex tables, July 2020, 10-year minimum guaranteed pay, 2% annual indexation for illustration purposes only. Annuity rates change frequently. Please obtain the latest rates before doing your calculations.

10.12 The Income Zones

You can categorize your financial position into one of the three "zones": green zone, gray zone, and red zone.

10.12.1 Green Zone

If the required withdrawals are lower than SWR, then you are in the green zone. This means, there are sufficient assets to finance the retirement income, as well as the luck factor throughout retirement.

Furthermore, if your assets are large enough to pass various stress tests as well, then you are in the deep-green zone.

What are the implications of being in the green zone?

- **Luck:** Luck is not important; you have sufficient savings to cover the luck factor.
- **Focus:** Once the retirement plan is in place, then cash flow planning, retirement planning, and risk planning require very little additional time and energy. Pay more time and attention to estate planning, tax planning, investment planning, and portfolio costs on an ongoing basis.
- **Life annuity:** In the green zone, a guaranteed income is not necessary. Here, a life annuity is an *investment* decision and not an *insurance* decision. In a low-interest-rate environment, an annuity would be a bad investment decision.

10.12.2 Red Zone

If the required withdrawals are larger than what a life annuity would pay, then you are in the red zone. This means you have insufficient assets to cover the luck factor *and* insufficient assets to finance retirement income needs. You need to find ways of moving from the red zone into the green zone.

Some remedies are:

- delay retirement;
- work part-time after retirement;
- rent part of the home;
- buy lifelong guaranteed income (segregated funds or annuities, deferred or immediate);
- reduce spending;
- analyze when to start social security and any other pension income;
- plan on selling other non-essential assets (cottage) when needed;
- consider downsizing the existing home; or
- combination of any of the above.

What are the implications of being in the red zone?

- **Luck:** The financial drain on retirement assets is too high, therefore luck cannot help in a significant way.

- **Focus:** Pay more time and attention to cash flow planning, retirement planning, and risk planning. Do not spend too much time on estate planning, tax planning, investment planning, and portfolio costs until these issues are fixed. Your priority should be finding ways of moving into the green zone.

- **Life annuity:** In the red zone, a life annuity is an *insurance* decision and not an *investment* decision. You need annuities to ensure lifelong income, regardless of prevailing interest rates.

10.12.3 Gray Zone

If the required withdrawals are lower than what a life annuity would pay but higher than SWR, then you are in the gray zone. This means that assets are sufficient to finance retirement income, but insufficient to finance the luck factor. The major difference between the red zone and the gray zone is this: In the red zone, you have insufficient lifelong income, even after buying a life annuity. In the gray zone, you can have sufficient lifelong income if you use part of your assets to buy a life annuity.

Try to move from the gray zone to the green zone using remedies suggested for the red zone. If you are still in the gray zone, you should consider life annuities or segregated funds with lifelong income guarantees (variable annuities) to cover essential and basic expenses.

What are the implications of being in the gray zone?

- **Luck:** If income is generated from investment assets (and not annuities), then luck will play a large impact on the outcome;

- **Focus:** Pay more time and attention to cash flow planning, retirement planning, and risk planning to bring you into the green zone. Do not start the estate planning process until the retirement income issue is completely solved.

- **Life annuity:** to buy or not to buy a life annuity is an *insurance* decision and not an *investment* decision. In the gray zone, you need it. Annuities, as well as segregated funds with lifelong income guarantees, are suitable.

Figure 32 shows the zones for a 65-year-old male with $1 million of retirement assets.

Figure 32: Green, gray and red zones of retirement income

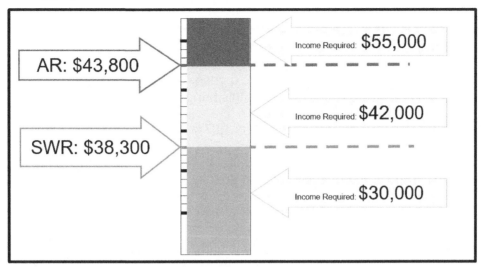

On the left-hand side of the column, the SWR is the border between the green zone and gray zone. The annuity payout amount (AR) is the border between the red zone and the gray zone.

- If he needs $55,000 per year which is larger than what the annuity would pay), then he is in the red zone.

- If he needs $42,000 per year which is between the annuity payout and SWR), then he is in the gray zone.

- If he needs $30,000 per year, which is less than the SWR), then he is in the green zone.

Here, the sustainable amount is indexed to CPI. The annuity payout is indexed only by 2% annually, which is what is available in the market currently.

Let's look at an example:

> **Example:** Cindy, 65, is just retiring, with no dependents. She has $750,000 in her buy-and-hold retirement portfolio. After taking into account all her income from other sources (government benefits, rental income, etc.), she needs $10,000 per year from her savings for essential expenses, $15,000 per year for basic expenses, and $6,000 per year for discretionary expenses. Does she have enough savings?
>
> Essential Expenses: Divide $10,000 by the SWR, 3.10% (see Table 17), to calculate how much assets are required: $10,000 / 0.0310 = $322,581
>
> Basic Expenses: Divide $15,000 by the SWR, 3.83% to calculate how much assets are required: $15,000 / 0.0383 = $391,645
>
> Discretionary Expenses: Divide $6,000 by 4.65% to calculate how much assets are required for discretionary expenses $6,000 / 0.0465 = $129,032
>
> Cindy needs $843,258 in total retirement assets, calculated as $322,581 + $391,645 + $129,032. Her retirement assets are insufficient to cover all her income needs.

Let's consider a life annuity:

> **Continuing with the previous example:**
>
> Cindy is inflexible about her retirement expenses but is open to life annuities for her essential and basic income needs. Can this bring her into the green zone?
>
> The annuity rate for a female at age 65 is 4.07% (from Table 27)
>
> Essential + Basic Expenses: Divide $25,000 by the annuity rate of 4.07%, to calculate how much assets are required to buy an annuity: $25,000 / 0.0407 = $614,251
>
> Discretionary Expenses: No change, it is still $129,032
>
> The total amount of assets required for lifelong income is $743,283, calculated as $614,251 to buy a life annuity plus $129,032 investment assets for discretionary expenses.
>
> Cindy has $750,000 of retirement assets. This is slightly more than what she needs for lifelong income, only if she chooses to buy a life annuity to cover her shortfall of essential and basic expenses.
>
> Before considering the life annuity, Cindy was in the gray zone. Now she is in the green zone.

10.13 Conclusions

A good understanding of SWR is the key to retirement income planning. SWR tables for various asset allocation strategies presented in this Chapter can help you answer the most critical questions. In addition, you can stress-test the impact of differing longevity and withdrawal needs, as well as portfolio underperformance and higher future inflation.

The highest priority should always be moving from the red or gray zone into the green zone. If this is not possible, then consider annuities. When buying life annuities, ladder them over three or four years. This can reduce the interest rate risk. Alternately, instead of "buying" lifelong guaranteed income through a life annuity and giving up your assets, you can "rent" lifelong guaranteed income through a variable annuity without giving up your capital, but paying fees on an ongoing basis.

11 Managing the Inflation Risk

In this chapter, we will discuss the additional capital required to mitigate inflation risk for annuities or pensions that are not fully indexed to CPI.

Many retirement planners use a 2% CPI indexation. This contradicts the fact that inflation was larger than this number 60% of the time since 1900. It was greater than 4% about 28% of the time and significantly greater than that many times in the past. Furthermore, recent spikes in inflation make a 2% assumption no longer feasible. We cannot be complacent about it.

Life annuities and pensions eliminate longevity and market risks, but they do not necessarily eliminate the inflation risk. Many do not come with full CPI indexation or any indexation at all.

Let's work with some numbers to clarify the inflation risk. Say, a pension pays $10,000 per year, indexed by 1% per year for life, starting at age 70. During the first year, it pays $10,000. No problem there, except CPI was 3.2% for that year. In the second year, the retiree needs $10,320 to maintain his purchasing power. However, the pension payment goes up by 1% to $10,100. Now, we have an "indexation shortfall" of $220 during the second year.

To make up for this shortfall, we need a separate "inflation bucket". This is only for calculation purposes and in real life, this bucket can be part of any other portfolio.

How much you need in this inflation bucket is calculated using an "asset multiplier". This asset multiplier indicates how many dollars of savings you need for each dollar of annual income from that pension or annuity. Tables 28 through 30 indicate the asset multipliers for different retirement ages and indexation methods.

Inflation buckets are necessary only when this income is required to pay for essential and basic expenses. You do not need an inflation bucket in the following circumstances:

- if income from an annuity or a pension is used to pay discretionary expenses,
- if you take the income from an annuity or a pension and then add this to your savings,
- if a pension or annuity income is indexed fully to CPI.

To make sure that the inflation bucket is as reliable as the underlying income stream, we calculated these asset multipliers for a 0% historical failure rate for the entire retirement time horizon.

11.1 Asset Multipliers

We cover here three of the most popular indexation methods: fixed, partial, and differential. There are other methods followed by some pension plans; such as conditional or performance-based. We do not cover them here because they require inputs that are specific to each pension, and that is beyond the scope of this book.

11.1.1 Income Streams with Fixed Indexation

A fixed indexation means that the income is indexed annually by a fixed amount each year. Table 28 shows the asset multiplier to calculate the inflation bucket for income streams with 0%, 1%, and 2% annual indexation[17].

Table 28: Asset multiplier for an annuity or pension income with fixed indexation for life

Retirement Age	Asset Multiplier		
	Income stream is indexed by 0%	Income stream is indexed by 1%	Income stream is indexed by 2%
60	13.2	11.9	10.3
65	11.9	10.6	9.2
70	10.3	9.2	8.0
75	8.3	7.5	6.7
80	6.3	5.7	5.1

If you have fixed indexation, you might sometimes have a surplus of income. For example; if the annuity payment is indexed each year by 2%, but CPI was only 0.5% during last year, then you have a surplus this year. All figures in Table 28 are based on any such surplus amounts being deposited back into the inflation bucket (and not spent).

11.1.2 Income Streams with Partial Indexation

A partial indexation is when the annual indexation of a pension or annuity payment is a portion of the actual CPI, such as half of the CPI. Table 29 shows the asset multiplier to calculate the inflation bucket for income streams that are indexed by 30% of CPI, 50% of CPI, and 70% of CPI.

Table 29: Asset multiplier for an annuity or pension income, indexed partially for life

Retirement Age	Asset Multiplier		
	Income stream is indexed by 30% of CPI	Income stream is indexed by 50% of CPI	Income stream is indexed by 70% of CPI
60	10.5	8.2	5.4
65	9.4	7.3	4.8
70	8.1	6.2	4.1
75	6.4	4.9	3.2
80	4.8	3.6	2.3

---

[17] An annuity with 0% indexation is also called a flat annuity or a straight annuity.

11.1.3 Income Streams with Differential Indexation

A differential indexation is when the annual indexation of a pension or annuity payment is less than the actual CPI by a fixed amount. For example; "CPI less 2%". That means when CPI is 3.5%, the pension payment is indexed by 1.5% for that year. It also means when CPI is 2% or below, there is no indexation, and the pension income stays the same. Table 30 shows the asset multiplier to calculate the inflation bucket for income streams that are indexed by CPI less 1%, CPI less 2%, and CPI less 3%.

Table 30: Asset multiplier for an annuity or pension income, indexed differentially for life

Retirement Age	Asset Multiplier		
	Income stream is indexed by CPI less 1%	Income stream is indexed by CPI less 2%	Income stream is indexed by CPI less 3%
60	3.3	6.0	8.3
65	2.9	5.3	7.4
70	2.3	4.3	6.1
75	1.8	3.3	4.6
80	1.1	2.1	3.0

Example: Jeremy and Claudine are both 70, just retiring.

Income from other sources: Their combined government retirement benefits are $34,000 per year. In addition, Claudine has a pension that pays $22,000 per year, indexed to half of CPI annually. Jeremy has a life annuity that pays $13,000 per year with no indexation.

Expenses: Their annual expenses are $100,000, of which $50,000 is for essential expenses, $40,000 is for basic expenses, and $10,000 is for discretionary expenses.

How much retirement assets do they need?

Inflation bucket for Claudine's pension: Lookup Table 29 for partial indexation, at age 70 and 50% of CPI. The asset multiplier is 6.2. They need an inflation bucket of $136,400, calculated as 6.2 × $22,000.

Inflation bucket for Jeremy's pension: Lookup Table 28 for fixed indexation, at age 70 and 0% indexation. The asset multiplier is 10.3. They need an inflation bucket of $133,900, calculated as 10.3 × $13,000.

...continued on the next page

With these two inflation buckets in place, they now have $69,000 per year income (calculated as $34,000 + $22,000 + $13,000), indexed to CPI for life. Now, we can calculate how much more assets they need.

Essential Expenses: Their $69,000 income from other sources (plus inflation buckets) pay their essential expenses of $50,000 in full. In addition, there is a surplus of $19,000 that we carry over towards meeting their basic expenses (calculated as $69,000 less $50,000). Jeremy and Claudine don't need any savings to meet their essential expenses.

Basic Expenses: Their basic expenses are $40,000. We carried over the surplus of $19,000 from income from other sources. This means they need to withdraw $21,000 from their retirement assets (calculated as $40,000 - $19,000) to cover their basic expenses.

The SWR for basic expenses: at age 70 is 4.34% (see Table 17). Divide $21,000 by 4.34% to calculate how much assets they need for their basic expenses: $21,000 / 0.0434 = $483,871

Discretionary Expenses: Their discretionary expenses are $10,000 per year. The SWR for discretionary expenses: at age 70 is 5.33% (see Table 17). Divide $10,000 by 5.33% to calculate how much assets they need for discretionary expenses $10,000 / 0.0533 = $187,617

The total amount of assets they need is $941,788, calculated as $136,400 (Claudine's inflation bucket) + $133,900 (Jeremy's inflation bucket) + $483,871 (for basic expenses) + $187,617 (for discretionary expenses).

11.2 Conclusions

Inflation has been relatively subdued for the last several years. Then came the pandemic with supply-side issues and labor shortages. The globalization of the last forty years has peaked and we start seeing some de-globalization activities. As if these are not enough, military conflicts are straining currency and food supply balances further. In late 2021 and early 2022, inflation started making 40-year highs.

The asset multiplier tables presented in this Chapter can help you estimate how much retirement assets you will need if you have income from other sources that are not fully indexed.

12 Income Allocation

In this chapter, we will cover income allocation. In Chapters 10 and 11, we worked on examples that involved income allocation techniques. Here, we expand the concept with more details and examples.

12.1 Income Allocation

Let's first recap how asset allocation and income allocation work together.

Asset allocation limits the impact of volatility on the portfolio's value. It works on the vertical axis of the forecast chart, the dollar dimension (see Figure 18). It is an effective tool in "normal" times. However, its benefit during "fractal" times is limited.

When we talk about asset allocation, we visualize it with pie charts (Figure 33). On the pie chart, we show how much is allocated to different asset classes/groups. Generally, the asset mix does not change much, except for specific life events that might necessitate temporary adjustments for specific cash flow situations.

Figure 33: An example of an Asset Allocation Chart

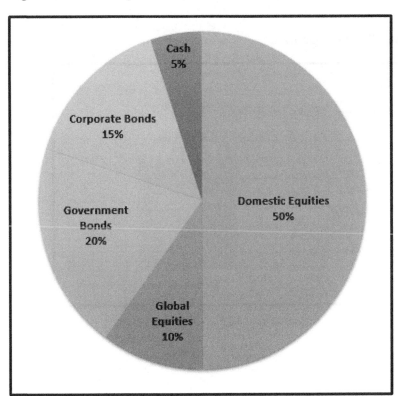

Income allocation is the process of deciding which income source pays for what category of expenses (essential, basic, and discretionary). It provides the baseline for income and expenses. We can then use it for different stress test scenarios.

Income allocation affects the horizontal axis of the forecast chart, the time dimension (see Figure 18). It limits the adverse impact of luck on a portfolio's longevity. While asset allocation works best in normal times, income allocation works well in fractal times. In other words, asset allocation takes advantage of good luck, income allocation mitigates bad luck during retirement. Similar to the two fists of a boxer, they provide an effective, one-two counterpunch back at the luck factor. A well-designed income allocation strategy makes the retirement plan indestructible (almost).

During the discovery process, go over each expense item and categorize it as essential, basic, or discretionary. This takes a considerable amount of time. But it is time well spent. Once the income allocation is created, you don't need to revisit it until the next major life event.

We visualize income allocation with two vertical bar charts on the same graph (Figure 34). The bar on the left represents income, such as social security retirement income (SSRI), pensions, rental income, royalties, savings, and so on. The bar on the right represents expenses: essential, basic, and discretionary. We then connect these two bars to reflect the money flow from income to expense. Note that, the pie chart for asset allocation shows percentages; the bar chart for income allocation shows dollar amounts.

Figure 34: An example of an Income Allocation Chart

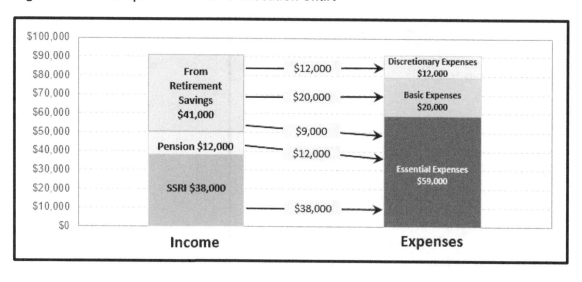

12.2 Planning Steps

The income allocation process has seven steps. Let's cover each one in detail using examples.

Step #1: Expected Income: Make a list of expected retirement income from all other sources, such as SSRI, pensions, annuities, rental income, business income, royalties, etc.

At this point, exclude all income from retirement investments, such as dividends, capital gains, interest income, return of capital, or portfolio growth. These are handled separately in Step #4.

Example (Step #1): Henry and Amina, both 70, just retired. They want income until age 96. This is their expected income during retirement.

Income Source:	Index	Henry	Amina	Total
SSRI	Full	$34,100	$28,400	$62,500
Pension A	2%	$0	$18,000	$18,000
Pension B	None	$14,000	$0	$14,000
Total		$48,100	$46,400	$94,500

Note that in this example, Amina's pension, Pension A, is indexed by 2% annually. Henry's pension, Pension B, is not indexed at all. Therefore, unless Henry and Amina have a surplus of income to start with, they will also need the inflation buckets that we discussed in Chapter 11.

Step #2: Expected Expenses: Make a list of all expected retirement expenses. Categorize it as essential, basic, or discretionary.

Example (Step #2): Henry and Amina go over their expenses and categorize them. Here is the list:

Expense Category:	Amount
Essential	$70,000
Basic	$30,000
Discretionary	$20,000
Total	$120,000

Step #3: Income Allocation Chart: Now, you can construct the income allocation chart.

On the expenses column (the vertical bar on the right-hand side), place the essential expenses first. Stack basic expenses above it, and then stack the discretionary expenses above the basic expenses.

On the income column (the vertical bar on the left-hand side), place guaranteed income from other sources at the bottom of the column, such as SSRI. Above these, stack pensions and income from other sources.

The first rule is that income and expenses must be equal. This means that both vertical bars must be of the same height. If the income column is shorter than the expenses column, then retirement savings cover this shortfall of income. Add a new box, "From Retirement Savings", to the top of the income column, making the height of the income column the same as the expense column (as in Figure 34). This is the shortfall that must be provided by your savings.

The second rule is that the retirement savings box should be always placed on **top** of all income from other sources.

It is also possible that the income column is taller than the expenses column. This happens when a retiree has a large pension, rental income, business income, or royalties. Here, we have a surplus of income. Add a new box, "Surplus", just above discretionary expenses to make the height of the expenses column the same height as the income column (Figure 35). All the surplus goes into this box. You can do whatever you want with it; spend, donate, reinvest, or help children and grandchildren.

Figure 35: An example of an Income Allocation Chart with a surplus of income from other sources

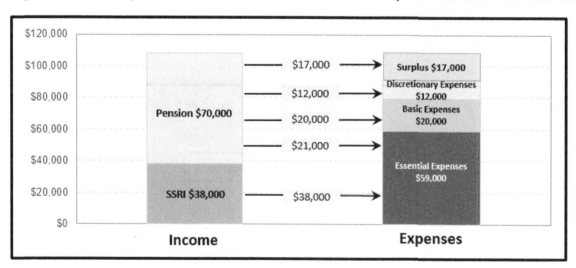

Let's continue with our example and create the income allocation chart for Henry and Amina.

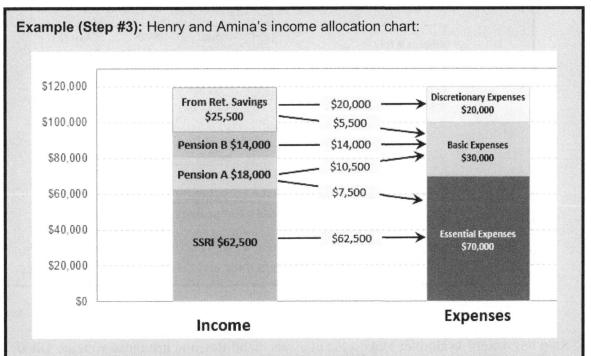

Example (Step #3): Henry and Amina's income allocation chart:

Income from other sources pays a total of $94,500 (SSRI, Pension A, and Pension B). They need $120,000. They have a shortfall of $25,500 which must be covered´by their retirement savings.

Step #4: Assets Required: Calculate assets required to cover the shortfall of retirement income and the inflation bucket. Here, we use the calculation methods we covered in Chapters 10 and 11.

Example (Step #4): Calculate how much retirement savings Henry and Amina need to have lifelong income.

To calculate the assets required to meet the shortfall of expenses, divide the dollar amount needed by the SWR (Chapter 10).

To calculate the assets required to cover the impact of inflation, multiply the annual pension income amount with the multiplier (Chapter 11).

…continued on the next page

What is it for?	Amount Needed	SWR (Table 17)	Assets Required
Essential Expenses	$0	3.46%	$0
Basic Expenses	$5,500	4.34%	$126,728
Discretionary Expenses	$20,000	5.33%	$375,235

	Amount to index	Multiplier (Table 28)	Assets Required
Inflation Bucket for Pension A	$18,000	8.0	$144,000
Inflation Bucket for Pension B	$14,000	10.3	$144,200
Total Retirement Savings Required:			**$790,163**

Henry and Amina need a total of **$790,163** in retirement savings in addition to their income from all other sources. This covers their expenses of $120,000 per year.

Step #5: Assets Available: Make a list of assets, liabilities, and insurance policies. Divide assets into two categories: assets available for retirement and all other assets.

Example (Step #5): Henry and Amina make a list of their assets:

Assets available for Retirement	Market Value
Henry - Retirement Savings	$630,000
Amina - Retirement Savings	$665,000
Bank Accounts	$36,000
Joint Investment Account	$430,000
Total Assets available for Retirement:	$1,761,000

Other Assets	Market Value
Principal residence	$1,120,000
Cottage	$530,000
Other Assets:	$1,650,000

Insurance	Coverage
Joint Life, first to die	$850,000

Step #6: Ask: Are the available assets larger than the required assets?

- If "yes": you have sufficient assets for lifelong income. Skip to step #7
- If "no": you have a shortfall of assets. Consider potential remedies: delay retirement, save more, spend less, downsize home, sell the home, rent part of the home, buy a life annuity, or work part-time after retirement. Revise the list of retirement expenses and assets and go to Step #1. Repeat until you are in the green zone.

> **Example (Step #6):** Henry and Amina have assets worth $1,761,000 to meet their retirement income needs.
>
> They calculated in Step #4 that they need $790,163.
>
> Therefore, they have sufficient assets for lifelong income. They are in the green zone.

Step #7: Stress Tests: Analyze all stress points, and find all weaknesses of the base plan. Document all findings and considerations for future reference.

Some of the stress test points occur at major life events:

- underperformance of portfolio, higher inflation (see the SWR tables for stress test);
- death of the spouse;
- the potential need for long-term care for one or both spouses;
- living beyond the age of death that was assumed in the plan;
- increased essential and basic expenses;
- care for surviving, disabled dependents; and
- any other situation that might need a stress test analysis.

The following pages show examples of stress tests for Henry and Amina.

Market Underperformance:

> How much Henry and Amina would need using the stressed sustainable withdrawal rates?
>
> To calculate the assets required to meet the shortfall of expenses, divide the dollar amount needed by the stressed SWR (Chapter 10).
>
> The inflation buckets remain the same.
>
> *...continued on the next page*

What is it for?	Amount Needed	SWR (Table 18)	Assets Required
Essential Expenses	$0	2.99%	$0
Basic Expenses	$5,500	3.79%	$145,119
Discretionary Expenses	$20,000	4.63%	$431,965

	Amount to index	Multiplier (Table 28)	Assets Required
Inflation Bucket for Pension A	$18,000	8.0	$144,000
Inflation Bucket for Pension B	$14,000	10.3	$144,200
Total Retirement Savings Required:			**$865,284**

Henry and Amina need a total of **$865,284** to cover their expenses of $110,000 per year under stressed market performance.

They have sufficient assets for lifelong income under stressed market conditions.

Stress-Test Death of a Spouse:

Henry dies the next day. What now?

For stress-testing the death of one spouse, repeat steps #1 through #6 for the surviving spouse using the new figures for income, expenses, and assets.

Expected Income:
Henry's pension (Pension B) pays 60% to the surviving spouse. For the sake of simplicity, we ignore any survivor benefit from Henry's SSRI.

Income Source:	Index	Henry (deceased)	Amina	Total
SSRI	Full	$0	$28,400	$28,400
Pension A	2%	$0	$18,000	$18,000
Pension B	None	$8,400	$0	$8,400
Total		$8,400	$46,400	$54,800

...continued on the next page

Expected Expenses:

After Henry's passing, Amina's expenses are as follows:

Expense Category:	Amount
Essential	$65,000
Basic	$25,000
Discretionary	$20,000

Construct Income Allocation Chart:

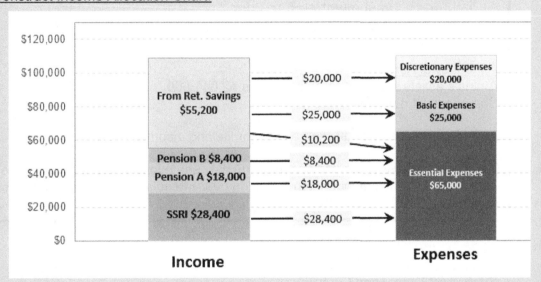

Calculate Assets Required:

What is it for?	Amount Needed	SWR (Table 17)	Assets Required
Essential Expenses	$10,200	3.46%	$294,798
Basic Expenses	$25,000	4.34%	$576,037
Discretionary Expenses	$20,000	5.33%	$375,235

	Amount to index	Multiplier (Table 28)	Assets Required
Inflation Bucket for Pension A	$18,000	8.0	$144,000
Inflation Bucket for Pension B	$8,400	10.3	$86,520
Total Retirement Savings Required:			**$1,476,589**

...continued on the next page

Assets Available for retirement expenses:

Henry's retirement savings are transferred to Amina. All other assets remain the same, plus $850,000 which is the proceeds of the life insurance.

Assets available for Retirement	Market Value
from Henry's Retirement Savings	$630,000
Amina - Retirement Savings	$665,000
Proceeds of life insurance	$850,000
Bank Accounts	$36,000
Joint Investment Account	$430,000
Total Assets available for Retirement:	$2,611,000

Adequacy of Assets:

Amina's assets available for retirement is $2,611,000.
She needs $1,476,589.

Therefore, Amina has sufficient assets for lifelong income.

To maximize her income and minimize the risk, she might consider buying either a life annuity or a variable annuity with a lifelong guaranteed income to cover her essential expenses.

Stress-Test Long-Term Care:

Henry moves to a long-term care facility at age 88. Amina stays at home. Henry dies while there at age 93. In current dollars, the long-term care facility costs $80,000 a year, and this cost goes up by 4% each year.

For this type of scenario, doing these calculations by hand is complicated. It is much easier to plug numbers into the aftcast spreadsheet and observe the portfolio value.

Here is the aftcast for this scenario:

…continued on the next page

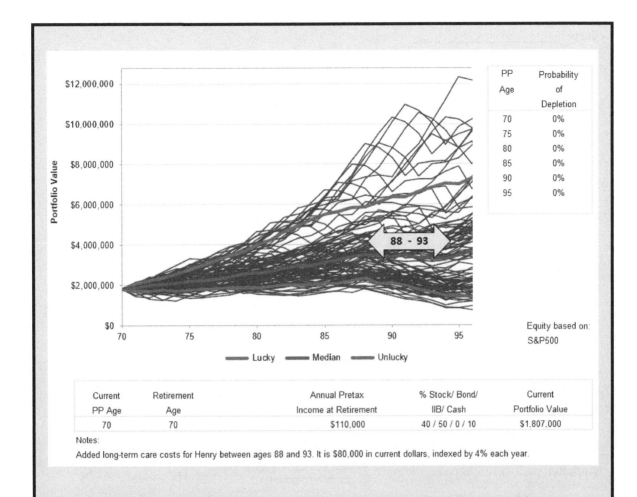

PP Age	Probability of Depletion
70	0%
75	0%
80	0%
85	0%
90	0%
95	0%

88 - 93

Equity based on: S&P500

Lucky — Median — Unlucky

Current PP Age	Retirement Age	Annual Pretax Income at Retirement	% Stock/ Bond/ IIB/ Cash	Current Portfolio Value
70	70	$110,000	40 / 50 / 0 / 10	$1,807,000

Notes:
Added long-term care costs for Henry between ages 88 and 93. It is $80,000 in current dollars, indexed by 4% each year.

This aftcast chart* shows that historically, even in the worst-case scenario, Henry and Amine have sufficient assets to cover all their expenses. And if they experience a worse future performance than shown here on the aftcast, they can sell their cottage to raise cash.

Henry and Amina passed all our stress tests with flying colors. Therefore, they are in the deep green zone.

* using the Single Asset version of aftcast spreadsheets

12.3 Conclusions

Income allocation is an essential part of retirement income planning. Just like asset allocation, once it is set in place, you don't have to think about it until there is a major life event.

Retirement Cash Flow Worksheet and Budget

Date: _____

Part 1: Retirement Income Estimation Worksheet:

Notes: 1. Do not include below withdrawals from your investment/retirement portfolios

2. Include both spouse's income if married

	Annual Income $	CPI Indexed? ☑	
Continued Employment of Spouse	_____	☐	(Until Age: _____)
Part Time Employment	_____	☐	(From Age: _____ Until: _____)
Part Time Employment	_____	☐	(From Age: _____ Until: _____)
Pension Plan:	_____	☐	(From Age: _____ Until: .)
Pension Plan:	_____	☐	(From Age: _____ Until: .)
Pension Plan	_____	☐	(From Age: _____ Until: .)
Annuity:	_____	☐	(From Age: _____ Until: .)
Annuity:	_____	☐	(From Age: _____ Until: .)
Government Benefits - Own: Social Sec..	_____	☐	(From Age: _____)
Government Benefits - Own: Other	_____	☐	(From Age: _____)
Government Benefits - Spouse: Social Sec	_____	☐	(From Age: _____)
Government Benefits - Spouse: Other....	_____	☐	(From Age: _____)
Rental Income:	_____	☐	(From: _____ Until: _____)
Royalty Income:	_____	☐	(From: _____ Until: _____)
Other	_____	☐	(From: _____ Until: _____)
Other	_____	☐	(From: _____ Until: _____)

> **Total Income from Other Sources:** $ _____

Part 2: Retirement Expenses Estimation Worksheet:

	Essential Expenses Annual $	Basic Expenses Annual $	Discretionary Expenses Annual $

HOUSING EXPENSES:

	Essential	Basic	Discretionary
Mortgage			
Rent paid			
Condominium Fees			
Property Insurance			
Property Tax			
Heating			
Water			
Electricity			
Security & Alarm			
Maintenance			
Repairs			
HOA			
Other:			
Other:			

HOUSEHOLD AND LIVING EXPENSES:

	Essential	Basic	Discretionary
Food, Groceries			
Dry Cleaning & Laundry			
Decorating & Painting			
Carpet Cleaning			
Gardening			
Pool Care			
Pet Care			
Kennel			
Maid Service			
Computer Equipment & Maintenance			
Pocket Money			
Clothing			
Footwear			
Dependent Support 1			
Dependent Support 2			
Gifts			
Donations			
Other:			
Other:			
Other:			

PAGE SUBTOTAL:			

	Essential Expenses Annual $	Basic Expenses Annual $	Discretionary Expenses Annual $

TRANSPORTATION EXPENSES:

Car Loan Payments			
Lease Payments			
Maintenance & Repairs			
License Fees			
Fuel			
Oil Change			
Parking			
Tickets			
Car Insurance			
Car Rental			
Public Transportation			
Other:			
Other:			
Other:			

INVESTMENT AND INSURANCE EXPENSES:

Investment Loan Payments			
Professional Fees: Accounting			
Professional Fees: Legal			
Professional Fees: Other			
Subscriptions			
Insurance Premiums 1			
Insurance Premiums 2			
Insurance Premiums 3			
Insurance Premiums 4			
Other:			
Other:			
Other:			

PAGE SUBTOTAL:			

	Essential Expenses Annual $	**Basic** Expenses Annual $	**Discretionary** Expenses Annual $

PERSONAL AND HEALTH CARE EXPENSES:

	Essential	Basic	Discretionary
Hair Care			
Beauty Supplies			
Personal Care			
Manicure, Pedicure			
Doctors			
Dentists			
Prescription Drugs			
Nutritional Supplements, Vitamins			
Visiting Home Care			
Live-in Home Care			
Medical & Support Equipment			
Other:			
Other:			
Other:			

COMMUNICATION EXPENSES:

	Essential	Basic	Discretionary
Telephone			
Mobile Phone			
Cable TV			
Satellite TV			
Pay TV			
Internet			
Other:			
Other:			
Other:			

PAGE SUBTOTAL:			

	Essential Expenses Annual $	**Basic** Expenses Annual $	**Discretionary** Expenses Annual $

RECREATIONAL AND ENTERTAINMENT EXPENSES:

Club Memberships			
Travel			
Camping			
Sports Equipment			
Books			
Newspapers			
Adult Education			
Hobbies			
Dining Out			
Entertaining at Home			
Theatre, Ballet, Concerts			
Sports Events			
Tobacco, Alcohol			
Other:			
Other:			
Other:			

ESTIMATED INCOME TAXES:

Income Taxes	
Other:	
Other:	
Other:	

PAGE SUBTOTAL:			

	Essential Expenses Annual $	**Basic** Expenses Annual $	**Discretionary** Expenses Annual $
TOTAL EXPENSES: (add all page subtotals)			

TOTAL EXPENSES (add: essential + basic + discretionary expenses): $ _____

Other Potential Expense Considerations:
- Buy a car every ____ years starting at age ____ until age ____.
- Increase Health Care Expenses by $ ____ after age ____.
- Increase Health Care Expenses again by $ ____ after age ____.
- Decrease Travel expenses by $ ____ after age ____.
- Sell house at age ____
- Move to nursing home at age ____

Part 3: Retirement Assets:

List all investments, such as CDs, GICs, bank accounts, retirement savings/income accounts and all assets that you will or you can withdraw income from during retirement. Include both your and your spouse's assets.

Do not include your primary residence, cottage, rental properties, personal items, hobby-related valuable items in the retirement assets section.

RETIREMENT ASSETS:	Current Market Value

Total Retirement Assets available: $ _____

OTHER ASSETS:	Current Market Value
Home	
Cottage	
Rental Property	
Rental Property	
Rental Property	

13 Additional Resources

For further information on topics discussed in this book, you can refer to the following publications:

- Otar, Jim C., "Unveiling the Retirement Myth", www.retirementoptimizer.com
- Nassim Nicholas Taleb, "The Black Swan – The Impact of Highly Improbable, Random House, 2007
- Edward R. Dewey & Og Mandino, "Foundation for the Study of Cycles", July 1998 (http://cycles.memberlodge.com/)
- National Bureau of Economic Research, "U.S. Business Cycle Expansions and Contractions", (www.nber.org/cycles.html)
- Nicholas Metropolis (1987), "The Beginning of the Monte Carlo Model", Los Alamos Science (1987 special issue)

Made in United States
North Haven, CT
25 April 2023

35869865R00059